Charles, keep up the good work!

Joan Dunning

THE LOON
Voice of the Wilderness

THE LOON

VOICE OF THE WILDERNESS

Written and Illustrated by Joan Dunning

Houghton Mifflin Company / Boston

DEDICATION

For my mother, who taught me respect for the written word and love for the beauty of nature, and who has shown, by example, the value of approaching impossible situations with a low center of gravity.

For information about permission to reproduce selections from this book, write to Yankee Books.

Published by arrangement with Yankee Books, Inc., Camden, Maine 04843.

Library of Congress Cataloging-in-Publication Data

Dunning, Joan.
The loon : voice of the wilderness / written and illustrated by Joan Dunning.
p. cm.
Reprint. Originally published: Dublin, N.H. : Yankee Books, © 1985.
Includes bibliographical references.
ISBN 0-395-59301-8
1. Common loon — Behavior.   I. Title.
QL696.G33D86   1991   91-13728
598'.442 — dc20   CIP

Printed in the United States of America

VB 10 9 8 7 6 5 4 3 2 1

Wild Columbine

Book design by Eugenie Seidenberg

ACKNOWLEDGMENTS

First of all, I must acknowledge my enormous debt to my husband, Peter, for taking me to that bald outcropping of rock on Cranberry Lake in the Adirondacks from which I first heard loons calling. If he had known that this whole project was being conceived in the darkest recesses of my mind as we sat there beneath the stars, he might well have taken me somewhere else. A highly competent artist himself, Peter probably never intended to play midwife to someone else's creation, but, in light of the fact that we did sit there and that this endeavor was begun, he has been a true friend — cooking countless delicious meals, functioning as editor when there was no publisher, and providing moral support when perhaps neither of us saw any reason for hope.

Secondly, I must express my deepest thanks to my stepson, Jesse, for sharing nearly his entire childhood with a book which has been more work and less fun than the most demanding sibling. I thank him for his patience and for being quiet all the thousands of times he has had to tiptoe in a small house. And, I want to thank him, too, for his advice, which, when asked for, has always reflected an exceptional artistic sensibility.

I'd like to express my sincerest thanks to Mike Whelan for the way he has come in and so adequately taken my place on our farm so that I could be free to finish this book.

Special thanks to Scott Sutcliffe, trustee of the North American Loon Fund, formerly with the Loon Preservation Committee, for reading the manuscript for accuracy, for supplying me with information and photographs, and for taking me with him during his work with loons on Squam Lake, New Hampshire.

Thanks to Rich and Judy Frutchey, who so generously helped me to go public with this project, without whose professionalism this book might not have seen the light of day.

Finally, thank you to the editorial staff at Yankee Publishing Incorporated (and in particular my editor, Sandy Taylor) for their almost instant enthusiasm for this book, and for their light-handed and respectful manner of dealing with its author.

Joan Dunning
Springfield, Vermont

CONTENTS

FOREWORD

As backwater pools go, it wasn't much — a tidal pool a couple of yards across and only a few inches deep, but it was its own little universe and I was captivated by its activity. So many tiny creatures that I'd never seen before — shellfish attached to the rock on one end, but open and obviously alive on the other; a short, squat thing with waving fronds on top that snapped closed when I probed them with a stick; dozens of dark stubby darters similar to but not exactly like polywogs; a small starfish inching ever so slowly along the bottom; a faster-paced crab, whose posture of defense with an inch-long claw would have seemed ludicrous to anyone other than the youngster who watched with a curious mixture of fascination and detachment.

In spite of the decades that have passed, the scene is every bit as clear as if I were watching a film. No, more than that. I can recall the familiar warmth of the sun on my back, the surprising warmth of the water, and how the rough grip of the rock turned quickly slippery under the surface of the pool. I can see the shifting play of sunlight on the mottled bottom, the never-quite-round circles of lemon-white light rippling in ceaseless motion through the moss green and granite-sandy grey. Even now the memory is mesmerizing.

I can feel the momentary stiffness just behind the knees when I straightened too quickly after squatting too long. I remember the sense of intense involvement, exploring, discovering, examining, analyzing. And then with the ingratitude typical of a growing boy, it was all tucked away; merely one more in a series of routine adventures. But for the eternity of a summer afternoon, that universe was mine, unfolding its mysteries just for me.

For everyone, there must be times like these, times when we become acutely aware of some special facet of the world in which we live: Watching with complete, breathless attention a spider spin its web. Times when we lose our sense of time, when we gladly abandon our ties to time in order to take a part in or become part of another phenomenon: Struggling with a chick as it pecks its way out of the shell. Our involvement transcends mere observation. We are caught up in the event — captivated by its quiet drama, savoring its intimacy. For some, the experience is so exhilarating that happenstance is not enough. It must be sought out. For a few, it becomes a way of life.

Joan Dunning is one such person. This is her book, and what a wonderful book it is! Wonderful in the sense of filled with wonder — that same kind of hungry, wide-eyed, childlike fascination, but with the mature analysis of the seasoned observer.

Joan Dunning brings to her book three dynamic talents. First, as an observer, with all that that word implies in clarity of perception and interpretation, in patience and perspicacity. Those who have tried can attest to the fact that just getting to see a loon is a challenge in itself. To be able to observe them intimately, while not transgressing on their territory or disturbing their way of life, is a feat worthy of special commendation.

Second, Joan Dunning is a writer with a facility for telling a story simply and accurately. She uses words easily. Her story line flows without artifice and seemingly without effort, and we are carried through an episode, through the seasons, through a life cycle as easily as from word to word. Third, as is readily seen, she is also a gifted artist, capturing in patient detail the spirit of her subject.

There is another, less tangible, but no less real or important aspect of Joan Dunning's talent — and that is her sensitivity. In a world where everyone professes to be an environmentalist, even those most guilty of exploitation, there are relatively few who do much more than talk about their involvement. Public understanding and awareness of environmental problems are grow-

ing. Publicity concerning such imminent dangers as deforesta-
tion, acid rain, toxic waste, and other pollutants is increasing.
But the social, economic, and technological forces that underlie
environmental problems are also multiplying. Without an
abrupt change of direction, the natural resources in large parts
of the world will continue to be degraded. (Calling attention to
the perils has become very fashionable, but crying out "Danger"
is still surprisingly unpopular.) There are some for whom debate
is not enough — some who choose their own way to call attention to the peril and point out the direction of a remedy. One can
only admire the manner in which Joan Dunning portrays the
problems and then allows us to draw our own conclusions.

Her subject is the loon. It is also a symbol, and a very
compelling one. No one of us who has ever heard the eerie call of
this symbol of the wilderness can ever remain undisturbed, nor
can we forget the first time.

For me, the first time was, as it probably has been for so
many others, a singular, memorable occasion. I was in my early
teens, working as a topper at a lumberjack camp in the northern
New England woods. It was a moonless night, and I had gone
but a short way along the path, breathing deeply of the cool mist.
At first I thought a woman screamed, or maybe laughed. Then it
happened again, the high-pitched tremolo, and it sounded more
like a baby crying, only that wasn't it exactly. I had a feeling as
though someone were brushing a feather up the back of my
neck. The third time, it was wilder, more insane, and seemed
much closer. I don't remember running, but I do remember
bursting through the cabin door, breathlessly trying to pretend I
wasn't frightened as I explained to Pepe what I thought I had
heard. Pepe was a big, genial timberman, with an easy humor
and a strong French Canadian accent. "Oh, that's a loon," he
laughed. The way he pronounced "loon" didn't rhyme with
"n$\overline{oo}$n" or "m$\overline{oo}$n." The double "o" was more like that in

"bŏŏk" or "lŏŏk," and I repeated it just as he had said it. "A lŏŏn? What's a lŏŏn?" "Eez a bird. You wait — I show you." I found it hard to believe that any bird could be responsible for the sound I had heard, and it was a long time before I fell asleep that night, staring into the shadows of my room, listening to a sound repeated at unpredictable intervals, sometimes far in the distance, but often it seemed just outside the window.

It was two or three days later that Pepe called out to me from the shore of the lake, "Eh! Eez a lŏŏn!" I ran to look. There was nothing. "Where?" I asked. "Wait," said Pepe, and as I watched, suddenly where there had been nothing before, there was a bird bobbing on the surface as though he had been there all along, and then just as suddenly he disappeared. He didn't dive, he didn't fly — he just disappeared. "Where is it?" I cried. Again, Pepe said, "Wait." And even as he said it, the loon bobbed to the surface so far from where it had been before that I was certain it had to be another bird, or perhaps some unbelievable phantom of a bird. And as if responding to my thoughts, the bird, with very little movement of the head or beak, called those two distinctive notes that I now know to be a wail, trailing off a bit at the end. It was answered moments later, from some distant spot I could not see, by what I assume must have been its mate. And then it was gone again. With a characteristic big, broad smile, and a friendly cuff on my shoulders, Pepe said, "Lŏŏn!"

Robert J. Lurtsema

(Narrator of the record "Voices of the Loon," Mr. Lurtsema is an actor, poet, painter, and composer, as well as host and executive producer of National Public Radio's classical music program "Morning Pro Musica.")

PREFACE

When one speaks of "a loon," without reference to species, one generally means *Gavia immer* (*gah*-vih-ah *im*-mer), because it is the most familiar species, its range having the greatest overlap with human habitation. It is, in fact, the only loon that nests in the continental United States. It is a very noticeable bird, with its beautiful calls and striking summer plumage, and so it has become known as the Common Loon, though its presence on northern lakes is becoming increasingly *un*common.

Loons are not related to ducks or geese, but belong to their own distinct order, Gaviiformes. Within the genus *Gavia*, there are four species, the four types of loons:

Gavia immer — the Common Loon
Gavia arctica — the Arctic Loon
Gavia stellata — the Red-throated Loon
Gavia adamsii — the Yellow-billed Loon

Arctic Loon

The Arctic Loon, like the Common Loon, is black and white in summer, but the striping on its neck is not confined to horizontal triangles, and there is slightly more black in the feathers on its back. It is smaller than the Common Loon, and its bill is more delicate. It nests on the tundra and winters along the entire west coast of North America. Its call is a mere whistle.

Red-throated Loon

The Red-throated Loon is a considerably smaller bird than the Common Loon, with a lighter colored bill and a noticeably straighter neck. In winter, it could be confused with the Common Loon as both species are grey, but in summer it is obviously different, in that it has a russet patch on its throat and stripes running up the back of its head. Its call is a quacking sound. It nests in Canada and Alaska and winters along the east and west coasts of the United States.

Yellow-billed Loon

The Yellow-billed Loon very closely resembles the Common Loon except for its obviously yellow bill and slightly larger

Common Loon

size. It is little known, however, since it nests only on the tundra
and winters along the west coast of Canada.

But it is the Common Loon with which this book is concerned — the loon that has most often captured people's imaginations and whose fate is most intertwined with man's.

INTRODUCTION

There are a number of reasons why I chose to write a book
on loons and persisted at it for eight years, despite the interruptions that a working sheep farm presents each summer with
undeniable urgency. They were quite diverse reasons, and I have
a feeling some of them will never be completely within the grasp
of my consciousness. But this is the nature of loons. They appeal
to people on several levels — the purely factual, the visual, but
also the deeply and inexplicably mysterious. It is this latter
quality, enigmatic and disturbing, that has kept this book nagging me the way a book on sparrows might not have. It kept it
from being rationalized out of existence before it ever reached
print — "No one would be interested. It's not worth the effort"
— the fate of so many books that are abandoned soon after
conception. But this subject of loons, once it laid hold of me, has
owned me so possessively that even when I was far from my
studio I felt a continuous urgency to be drawing, writing, giving
shape on paper to these strange and unusual birds that may have
so few seasons left to exist.

Many people know what I mean about this haunting quality
of loons, because I see it in their faces when I mention the
subject. But people seldom put their feelings into words. There is
something too deep, too personal going on inside of them.
Sparrows, pigeons — they stay out there on their own two feet,
just birds, separate from our psyches. But people familiar with
loons get the loon inside them, like a totem, and it seems to make
a little dark gap in the smooth base of rationality we try to keep
for our thoughts.

Have you ever heard a loon? This is often how it all begins.
Deep in the night you may have been awakened from a heavy
sleep, feeling a little defenseless, so relaxed in your bed or
sleeping bag. The sound is often distant, coming from some

remote, inaccessible corner of a lake, yet there is a quality to the call so penetrating that it can wake the soundest sleeper. Perhaps you lay there and listened, woke the person next to you with, "Shhh, what's that?" or silently slipped from your warm covers and out the door into the dark night to stand alone on the shore of the lake, beneath the shadowy pines. There may have been a little breeze off the water . . . the scene is so often the same. At night, like sentinels people stand, called to attention from their beds to stand in the darkness, to listen, to absorb the wisdom from the air. Overhead the stars stretch to the horizon, dotting the blue-black sky like the delicate speckles on a loon's side.

And then it comes again — the call known as the wail — but you know no such term for it. Heard for the first time, it isn't neatly called by any name. It is a sensation up the spine, a chill to the skin, a creator of that little gap in the mind through which one sees eternity.

Then comes an answer, distant from the origin of the first call, a repetition of the howl that brings to mind no image so comfortingly familiar as that of a wolf. And then, from the first area of endless dark night the first caller is heard again. Back and forth. You watch the darkness like a slow tennis game, and you begin to realize this is conversation you're overhearing. How can a sound that has conveyed you past the stars to the edges of the universe mean nothing more than "Come take your turn on the nest"? Or *does* it? Who are these creatures, this mated pair, that communicate in such terms?

Then there is silence once more. You realize that you're cold, standing there with little on, and go back to bed. But you are never the same again, once you have heard a loon.

✻ ✻ ✻

This is what I have lived with, this haunting subject. Actual-ly, when I first began to study loons it was purely for visual

reasons. I was attracted primarily by the beauty of their patterns — the triangles on their necks that camouflage so perfectly with reflections on the water cut into triangles by the loons' wakes; the stripes on their breasts that do a positive/negative reversal and turn to spots on the black of the loons' backs; the checkerboard of black and white so hard to distinguish from the reflection of bright light on open water — all of this geometry fascinated me, and I intended to do a series of paintings.

At the same time, however, I began to actually observe loons in the Adirondacks. Being a native Californian, I was a latecomer to an awareness of loons in their summer range, when they are in their familiar black and white breeding plumage and give their characteristic calls. Loons winter off the coast of Southern California, but in dull grey plumage and in remote silence. The more I observed loons on lakes in the northern United States and heard their calls, and the more I began to read about them, the more I became involved with the real bird, there floating on the water, not just the flat image I could create in my studio with a brush and paint on paper. In fact, I even began to have a feeling, at that time, that there is a danger in having animals "on paper." It seemed to me too easy to let the loon slip from actual existence on this planet, the way the tiger has begun to, because we have its beautiful graphic patterns to play with on paper. I began to see that the artist or photographer could inadvertently fool people into believing that an animal is alive and well because we keep their pictorial counterparts so vividly alive before us.

Then a strange thing began to happen. Next to my drafting table, where I do most of my writing and painting, I had tacked up a photograph of a loon. Actually, there are photographs and drawings of loons tacked on the walls all around my studio, but this particular photograph happened to be at eye level next to the window out of which I am accustomed to gaze. It is a photograph of a loon on its nest, with its head turned sideways so that one mahogany eye looks straight into the camera. I put the picture up so I could study the patterns of the summer plumage. On the same page there is a nice view of the back of the loon. *I* put the page up so that *I* could study the loons, but what I was not prepared for was that this loon, with its mahogany eye, would begin to scrutinize *me*. Increasingly, when I would turn to look absently out the window, my gaze would be caught and I would find myself held eye-to-eye by this sobering dark face that seemed to know so much more than I.

That is when I began to feel an obligation to go into depth on a subject that I had intended to treat only visually, to use words as spokesperson for this creature beside me that knew songs more beautiful than I could ever sing. My rather absent gaze grew more intent against the penetrating stare of a commercially worthless bird, in its sixty-millionth year of existence, now endangered through much of its range. I felt like a newcomer, descendant of a race only a couple of million years old, yet the loon looked on me as someone with the language to speak to a highly materialistic and rational society. It asked me to speak not just of facts — of wing length, flight speed, and winter range — but it looked on me as an artist as well and asked me to speak of intangibles, to convey the value of the loons' beauty, of their calls, of their very age and authority as one of the oldest birds on earth.

So this, above all, is why I have written this book; not just to give you factual information, which in itself is interesting and critical to know if we are to take practical measures to save the loon, but also to try to convey the loon's magic, to offer defense to a bird that has the ability to awaken us to the greatest mysteries of existence — both the infiniteness of our own subconscious and the vastness of all we may never know about life on this earth. The loon is like a touchstone for our society, a test of who we are and what we value. If we give it room to coexist with us, then it will be not just a symbol of the mysterious in nature, but a symbol of our reawakening wisdom and humility.

*   *   *

But there is one other reason that I have written this book, unrelated to anything I have mentioned so far. I am thinking of a time fifteen years ago that, by its very contrast to the usual peaceful setting one associates with loons, has remained a continually nagging backdrop to my work on this book. For the scene, I go to my home state of California, to Santa Barbara. Picture a path leading down to a beach through eucalyptus trees — the time around noon, the month February, the year 1969. I walked down the path with a man who worked for a branch of the California Wildlife Service, a figure moving ahead of me with concern and importance evidenced in his stride and a large walkie-talkie slung over his shoulder, into which he periodically radioed his impressions.

The beach we walked to was just across the Santa Barbara Channel from Union Oil's Platform A. We could not see the derrick, obscured by fog offshore, but, as I remember, it was one of three. Normally the platforms looked only potentially menacing, like ponderous robots. But that day Platform A was beginning an invasion of sorts, stealthily, with abundant resources at its disposal. I don't think anyone had any idea what the coastline was in for. It was just the first day of what was to become the Santa Barbara Oil Spill. In the course of eleven days, one thousand gallons of oil every hour leaked out of a fissure at the base of the well. The oil covered the water for four hundred square miles, and for forty miles of beach the situation was the same as the one we then approached.

Once we were on the beach, the walk over the deep, clean,

Sanderlings

dry sand was poor preparation for the scene that unrolled like a scroll through the fog as we turned and walked at water's edge. Most apparent was the thick mat of oil on the ocean's surface. It calmed the waves like a straitjacket. It washed up on the beach and left a heavy, continuous smear of oil for yards above the waterline. The white water was brownish yellow and the boiling of it took on a threatening appearance as it advanced and retreated with the subdued action of the waves. Our shoes instantly became heavy with new black soles that thickened as we walked along.

What I really was not prepared to see, even though this was what we had come to check on, were all the birds — species I had come to consider friends, like the sanderlings that accompanied me on long walks in flocks of briskly stepping individuals that moved in and out with the waves and snatched crabs from the sand as we moved along. I found them washed up, isolated from their flocks, caught by the oil and beached, alive but idle. They were black like the sand, tar babies with bird heads turned in fear as we approached.

Then there were the less familiar species, the ones that normally stay offshore and remote, brought in by this leveler of all birds. The shearwaters — I think it hurt me most to see these up close, birds that normally seemed proud in their distant independence, that one saw from boats only, far offshore, with their wide, strap-like wings — these joined the tiny sanderlings on the beach. And then we came to a bird I didn't know — not a grebe, no kind of duck — a bird that, even coated with oil, had a beauty to its form, to the smooth shape of its large, rounded head and neck, a sort of peaceful quality about it that the angularity and gawkishness of grebes and cormorants could not convey in the most serene of conditions.

The bird lay there, just up from the water, its head lifted, its oval eyes watching us. We passed it by, as we had all the other

Shearwater

casualties, walked up the beach for probably two or three more miles of the same repetitious sight, and then headed back. As we reapproached this bird I was again struck by the beautiful curve of its head, its thick neck, and I impulsively decided to take the bird home, to rescue it from the oil. This was a futile thing to do, in hindsight, nothing but a symbolic gesture, but I stooped down, gathered the bird's feet neatly under it with one hand, hugged its body to me so it could not flap its powerful wings, and with the other hand kept a firm hold on its head so it could not reach me with its beak.

What could I have hoped to provide such a foreign creature with none of the same habits as my own? As soon as I set it down

For loons, as for all birds at sea, contact with an oil spill is all too often fatal.

on the bathroom floor, I knew how tragically ridiculous the whole situation was. The bird lay poised, watching, waiting, while its very complex order was being rapidly jumbled by oil.

The hundreds of volunteers who were at that moment mobilizing never dreamed that the attempted rescue would be anticlimactic and disappointing. At a local zoo cages were being emptied, permanent residents consolidated to make room for thousands of birds being tenderly removed from the beaches and brought in for cleanup and a little rest. The birds were washed with a detergent solution and dried, placed in appropriate pens by species, fed appropriate fish, and given water to drink. And there they stood or, in the case of the loons, lay down, like spectres, waiting. But they could not wait long enough. Out on the ocean, other volunteers, the National Guard, and Union Oil were frantically trying to sop up the oil with hay. One by one the birds quietly died, virtually all of them, from ingested oil and from pneumonia.

My loon fared no better. A farmer friend of mine happened to stop by and when he saw the large pools of crude oil the loon was producing instead of excrement, he flatly declared I was wasting my time. So that loon had its neck wrung like a common goose, and what I did with its body I don't remember. My friend probably dealt with it for me. What I was left with was a bathroom to clean up, my clothes to wash, and a little bit of wonder. I found myself asking, just vaguely, who was that bird? What was this magic I was left with from its shape and size and seeming tranquility of expression? It was years before I dealt with loons again, but that experience never left me, nor the curiosity about who and what it was that I had encountered.

PART I
The Year

WINTER–
On the ocean

Come with me. Imagine we walk on a cold beach in winter. It is foggy, evening. The fog condenses on our hair and clothing and we are wet as if it has been raining. You may be disappointed with this fog that obscures our view and isolates us in a cloud of grey. Don't be.

Through the fog, beyond the breakers — they are out there. Let the strength of your imagination penetrate the fog, feel it move past your face till the first of the loons comes into view. They are large grey birds, nearly indistinguishable from the fog, floating silently, their beaks parallel with the surface of the water. They have been out here all winter like this — never going ashore, never touching anything still or solid, accustomed to the motion of the waves as we are accustomed to the stillness of land, unfazed by the dampness and cold. Though we are uncomfortable after only a few hours, for them it has been only a few hours out of many, out of days and weeks and months that they have been on the sea.

Red Algae

I don't regret that it is foggy because this will give you a better picture of the contrast between the two halves of a loon's year. Now that you have been here and seen the setting, it will make it easier for me to paint a picture of loons on the ocean. And when the loons head inland in the spring to the northern lakes, the crisp sparkle of the water, the intense blue of the sky, and the sharp contrast of the black and white breeding plumage will be all the more apparent to you by comparison.

It is January. The beginning of our calendar year is a meaningless demarcation for birds, but we will begin in January because it is as good a place as any to cut in on a yearly cycle that will have no end but will merge, without interruption, into the next.

When the loons fly north to breed, I want to focus on just one pair of loons but now, in winter, this is next to impossible. The tidy family units one observes in the north are dispersed widely. Mated pairs that have bred together year after year may now be separated by hundreds of miles, wintering on entirely different stretches of coastline. Not until spring will the male and female of a pair, returning separately to a familiar lake, each seek out their familiar territory, find one another, and breed.

Now life on the ocean is much more diffuse and remote from human awareness. But let's begin in the evening, in January. The loons have gathered in a loose flock for the night. It is just after sundown, and the light is leaving the fog that settles in around them. The loons are drifting, simply floating, heads forward, feet paddling occasionally to maintain position. Now and then there is a flash of white as a loon rolls on its side, exposing its breast, waggling its foot in the air before settling for the night. Occasionally a loon rears up, flaps its wings, and resettles. As the greyness turns to night, a loon reaches back to preen and then simply tucks its beak and dozes. One by one other loons tuck their beaks beneath their wings. Somewhere above the fog and clouds there are stars, but the loons are blanketed by moisture.

At dawn the fog still has not cleared. It is heavy in the air, partially obscuring the loons from one another, condensing on their broad backs. But the loons are not likely to care. Water is their preferred element. As light seeps into the fog, the flock is

The familiar black and white patterns of the loon characterize it for only half of the year. In winter, the loon takes on shades of grey and brown, although its breast and underparts remain white. Adults acquire winter plumage during the autumn molt and retain it until spring. It is very similar to the grey plumage of juvenile loons.

drifting, preening, spreading their outer feathers with oil from a gland near the tail, passing the feathers through the bill to rezipper minute barbs, which lock together to form a waterproof covering over warm inner down. As the flock drifts and preens, one after another the loons drop their heads beneath the surface of the water and another world opens up below. The light penetrates from above, dimming as it descends, and the loons watch for fish to pass from obscurity into view before disappearing again into the depths.

Loons are, above all, divers. Agility at all other activities has been sacrificed for clean mobility beneath the surface of the water. Now, as the light increases, one by one the loons head nearer shore to fish for the day, peering as they go, cruising with their eyes just beneath the waterline. It takes little effort, once one of them spots a fish, to descend and catch it. While most birds have hollow bones that make flight easy, loons have solid bones, giving them a specific gravity closer to that of water. Thus while flying is difficult for loons, they can almost effortlessly drop at will and glide through the undersea canyons.

The duration and depth of loons' dives have always been a source of fascination for people. In addition to having solid bones, loons are able to increase their specific gravity further by compressing air from their lungs, plumage, and internal air sacs. Their legs are positioned far back near their tails, making walking virtually impossible, but enabling loons to kick into a dive and be upturned in a moment. With such excellent adaptation, reports of three-minute dives or dives to depths of one hundred and eighty to two hundred feet may not be surprising, but the longer dives could be the result of a trick on the loon's part: When in danger, the loon can surface with only its bill exposed, take a breath, and resubmerge unnoticed. The extreme depths reported by fishermen may be the result of loons being caught as fishing nets are being hauled up. But regardless of possible

When the loon peers, it lowers its head beneath the surface of the water, so that its eyes are below the waterline. It may swim a considerable distance in this way, scanning the depths for fish.

The head rub is another preening movement in which oil is removed with the bill from the uropygial gland at the base of the tail and rubbed over the back feathers. The head is then rubbed over the back so that it, too, is waterproofed.

For the sake of agility under water, the loon's legs are set far back near its tail, with the thigh in a horizontal position. Thus kicking into a dive is easy.

exaggerations, loons are comfortable at exceptional depths and spend much of their time under water, averaging dives of from a few seconds to as long as a minute.

The loons spend the day fishing, patrolling the relatively shallow water nearer shore. Once one of them spots a fish or locates an area it would like to explore, it leaves the surface of the water with a quick bob of the head and is gone, streaking downward like a torpedo. Loons are opportunistic feeders; that is, a loon will pursue most any fish of a reasonable size that swims into view as the loon descends. If a loon captures a fairly small fish, it will swallow it under water and look for another; but if it catches a larger or spiny fish or a crab, it will surface, turn the prey over or break it up if necessary, and then swallow it.

Twice daily, the incoming tides bring new fish shoreward, simplifying the loons' life on the sea. Compared with the summer months, when the loons must maintain large territories in order to feed themselves and their chicks on a static food supply, life now seems very basic. There is none of the loud calling used in territorial defense, or to contact mates over long distances. Now the daily life of each loon is like a simple breathing in and out, movement inshore to feed, to drift and doze by day, and, as darkness falls, the return to deeper water as a precaution against being washed ashore in the night.

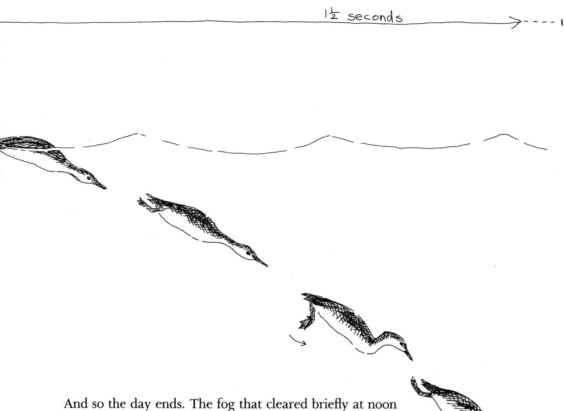

$1\frac{1}{2}$ seconds

And so the day ends. The fog that cleared briefly at noon settles in once more, re-creating a scene that will exist countless times over the winter. One by one the loons cease preening, waggle their feet and tuck them, put their heads over their backs, tuck their bills and sleep.

       *   *   *

But where does all this take place, you might be wondering, along what coastline? The setting is vague because it could be so many places — the Pacific coast, from the tip of the Aleutian

The Common Loon winters all along both coasts of North America, from as far north as the upper tip of the Aleutian Islands, to as far south as the southern tip of Florida. It is most commonly found along the Mid-Atlantic and Northeast coastlines, the eastern Gulf coast, and along the Pacific coast from southern California north to Vancouver Island. It also winters off the coasts of Norway and Great Britain, south to Algeria.

Islands all the way south to the Baja peninsula; the entire Gulf coast; the Atlantic coast, from Newfoundland south to Florida; the Great Lakes; and the entire west coast of Europe, from Scandinavia south to Algeria. It is believed that a loon breeding near the Pacific coast is apt to winter on the Pacific and one in the east is apt to winter on the Atlantic, while some of those in the middle will either go to the Great Lakes or funnel down a major river to the Gulf of Mexico, but what will actually be a particular loon's final destination in the fall is anyone's guess.

This is a source of frustration for the person who has spent the summer observing the comings and goings of a pair of loons. The joy one experiences when that pair appears with a newly hatched set of chicks makes fertile ground for despair when in winter there comes a report of an oil spill, with descriptions of massive loss of wildlife. If all one knows is that loons winter along the Atlantic coast, without knowing that for years the loons from a particular lake have been repeatedly found off Maine, for instance, then one spends an uneasy spring waiting to see if that certain pair will return to nest, or whether they were perhaps mired down in the oil and lost.

Unfortunately, this information is far from becoming available, and with good reason. Although the general shapes of migration patterns and winter ranges are easy to determine through observation, in order to trace the whereabouts of particular birds, one must band these birds and then retrieve the bands. This is what is done with most species of birds. They are netted and banded, then slowly the bands are returned by the general public, or the birds are renetted and the information is accumulated and synthesized.

But when a species of bird is already becoming scarce before people begin to get curious about it, and when that bird is as large and difficult to net as a loon, then biologists are reluctant to interfere. A further complication is that, because loons (in contrast to most ducks and geese, for instance) are no longer legally hunted, their bands do not readily fall into human hands, and when they do, the hands might be those of a hunter uneager to own up to the mistake. So very few loons ever get banded, and of those that do, scant information is returned.

Nevertheless, on the map of the winter range, it is interesting to note in what differing environments loons choose to winter. A loon off the Aleutian Islands will certainly encounter drastically different conditions from one off the coast of Florida. It seems that the motivation to migrate in the fall is due mainly to the need for open water on which to winter. This water need not be the ocean, as seen by the fact that loons winter on the Great Lakes. It simply must not freeze, regardless of how bitter the

The foot waggle is a comfort movement, during which the loon rolls to one side, exposing its white breast, extends a foot, and shakes it.

When a loon is dozing, its head is laid over its back and its bill is tucked between its wings. This posture may also be adopted when the bird is awake.

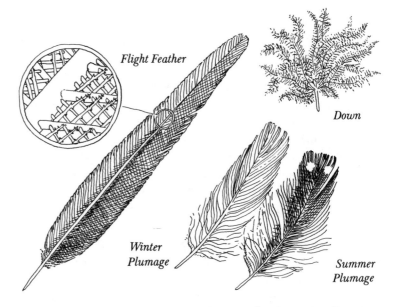

Flight Feather

Down

Winter
Plumage

Summer
Plumage

Loons, like most birds, are covered with warm down that is protected by an outer layer of contour feathers. Each of the contour feathers possesses a central shaft, to which are attached minutely barbed filaments. These barbs are zippered together as the feather is passed through the bird's bill during preening. Once zippered and oiled, the feathers form a watertight outer surface capable of shedding water, thus keeping the inner down absolutely dry. This is of vital importance for birds, particularly those that live on the water.

winter, and it must provide an adequate food supply till spring.

The fact that loons are able to exist on the ocean all winter is due to a number of adaptations common to most water birds. For instance, a loon is able to paddle with unfeathered feet through the iciest water due to a network of blood vessels in the upper legs, which reduces the temperature of the blood going to the lower legs, preventing heat loss and subsequent chilling. A loon's body is protected by a layer of subcutaneous fat, and further insulated by a thick layer of down, which in turn is encased in the dense, well-oiled layer of outer feathers. Without the thin, waterproof film that covers the outside of its feathers, a loon would have an experience on the winter ocean much the same as you or I would have — exposure to the cold water, exhaustion, pneumonia, and death.

And so the winter wears on . . . but perhaps this is inaccurate. I forget my human point of view. A lack of feathers, living

amidst considerable variety and entertainment is limiting. It is
hard to imagine dispensing with simple things like shelter and
solid ground (not to mention extravagant comforts like electric-
ity) and to imagine the open sea — the darkness at night, the
perpetual wetness, the continuous motion of the waves. Most of
us prefer warm, sunny days on shore when we can set up
brightly striped beach umbrellas and lie out on big towels, enjoying the feeling of the warm sand against our bodies. But perhaps
the loons prefer the air to reach its saturation point and the fog to
condense on their backs and drip off their bills. Perhaps the most
raging storms, with great rolling swells and howling winds, make
them feel the way we do on the sunniest of days. Perhaps with
water 360° around them, they bask in its profusion.

Bufflehead

　　　　　*　　　　　　*　　　　　　*

　　　As spring approaches, a change begins to come over the
birds on the ocean. The buffleheads, the goldeneyes perform
their courtship, the comical bobbing of their heads that makes
them look like toy ducks loose on the sea. Among the loons the
changes are more subtle, more internal, less visible, but there
nonetheless. They continue their feeding by day, patrolling the
coastline, diving for fish, drifting. But at night they are a little
slower to settle. Within each loon there is a growing feeling of
restlessness, an uneasiness, the gradual welling up of the same
undeniable energy that on land is filling the buds on the trees.
　　　The days have grown steadily longer. The equinox approaches, when day and night will be of equal length. After the
long winter, the sun itself now seems to have new force. It holds
off the twilight of evening, prolonging each day just a little bit,
encouraging the loons to fish just a little later. And when the
blue-grey of darkness finally does descend on the sea, the energy
absorbed from the afternoon's warmth seems to remain charged

Goldeneye

The wing flap is used to straighten the long flight feathers after the loon has either been underwater in a dive or has been preening.

in each loon. Preening goes on longer than usual. The loons rear up and flap their wings, stretching their muscles, feeling their strength. In the half-light the whites of breasts blink as loons here and there waggle their feet, tucking them to drift and then untucking them to paddle still longer in the twilight.

As the days pass, the spring molt gets underway. As if to increase each bird's capacity as a solar collector, in the early morning light, grey feathers, shed during the night's preening, are left floating on the water. In their place grow tiny black ones, first only on the cheeks of the adult loons, then spreading down their necks. Just as the darks and lights slowly emerge on a sheet of photographic paper when film is developed, so stripes and spots begin to replace the loons' muted grey with the emergence of white feathers among the black ones, and black feathers with white spots, in just the right combination, in just the right order to create the familiar patterns of the breeding plumage.

The time for the migration is approaching. For much of the winter the loons have been flightless. Unlike many birds that shed their wing feathers one at a time in order not to be grounded, loons are such heavy birds that they perhaps could not fly with even one of their long primaries missing. Thus, all the flight feathers are shed at once, on the ocean, when the tides bring the fish to the loons and flight is unnecessary. From January until March the loons undergo a molt of the wing feathers, which overlaps with the molt of the grey winter plumage. Thus, as the loons' newly emerged black feathers grow hot in the spring sunshine, so, hidden deep within the new plumage, along the blade of each wing, straight, stiff flight feathers too are growing — feathers strong enough to bear the weight of the heavy birds, strong enough to resist the air as the wings push down repeatedly in flight, strong enough to carry the loons the long way north.

The loons try their wings. They make short practice flights up and down the coastline, getting their muscles strong, picking up once more the rhythm of flight, getting used to the weight of their bodies suspended in air. But the time is not quite right. Whether from a sense of the angle of the sun or of the length of the days or from some inherited ability to calculate temperature and estimate the rate of thaw far away in the north, the loons remain poised, no longer settled, but balanced in time, waiting for the ocean to suddenly free them and the day to take them north.

In early spring the drab grey winter plumage is molted, and in its place grows the familiar black and white breeding plumage. This is acquired on the ocean, before the migration, at the same time that the flight feathers are renewed, ready for the long trip north.

SPRING – Migration

Hepatica

If you stopped to think about it, you might wonder why loons migrate.

Migration is a dangerous time for loons. To understand, you have only to picture the bird on solid ground. With its feet located far back near its tail, a loon is impossibly out of balance for walking. It moves only by pushing its belly along in an awkward sliding motion, and it is capable of doing this for only a few feet at a time.

Thus, the land is a potential trap for a loon. If, during migration, a loon for any reason finds itself on solid ground, whether because it grew tired and was unable to reach open water on which to rest, or because it might have mistaken wet pavement for a pond, then it is stranded. All of the adaptations that equip it for agility in the water — the position of its feet, its solid bones, its small wings — work against its getting airborne again. Shuffling and sliding over dry ground, over rocks, through brush is a highly inadequate way for a very heavy bird to pick up sufficient speed to fly. Loons often need as much as a quarter of a mile of open water over which to race with furiously beating wings in order to finally ascend.

Why do loons leave the ocean at all, where they are so capable of supplying their needs? Why head over land so alien

Spring migration can begin as early as late March and continue into June, depending on how far north an individual flies, and the rate of thaw in the north for that particular year. If spring is late, loons await warmer weather on the ocean before heading inland or pause on large bodies of fresh water. An average rate of progress puts loons off New York City in mid-April and off the coast of Maine in late April. On the West Coast, loons are off San Diego in March and April and off the coast of Washington state in April and early May, reaching Alaska in early to late May. Loons migrate by day, generally resting on the ocean, lakes, or rivers at night.

and dangerous, above cities and towns gleaming and threatening below, over factories with plumes of smoke clouding the air, above highways with tiny cars inching along, across miles of forest with trees a tangle of branches over dry ground?

For the good fishing, perhaps, that a lake can offer, newly released from the grip of the ice — but there is more to it than that. There is the matter of eggs. Fine for the fish in the ocean to leave theirs in the water behind them and swim on. Fine for the other birds that maneuver the land and air with ease to nest on rocky island rookeries at sea. But how does a bird that can manage only a few feet of travel overland, and that can neither alight safely on solid ground nor ascend from it, escape the reach of the tides and the ocean waves?

It flies inland, to calmer water. It may fly miles, for days and weeks over the land, to find that small bit of shoreline, those few feet of solid ground somewhere on the edge of a distant lake, which will cradle there among the stones or on a damp mat of sedge, two large, greenish brown, and speckled eggs.

＊   ＊   ＊

Toward the end of March, loons start moving up the coast from the south. Their presence on the water, the increased numbers of loons flocking, creates an excitement among the birds on the sea, a new watchfulness, a sensing of the weather, of conditions for flight, of air pressure and wind direction. The ocean no longer holds the loons. They seem only balanced there. They rear up on their tails and stretch their wings, arrange their feathers. Then, as the weather warms throughout the month of April, one by one and in small flocks, they take flight and begin the long trip north.

The loons will follow several general routes — along coastlines, along major rivers like the Mississippi, or overland, with an eye out for lakes on which to stop and rest and fish. The rate at which they make their way north depends not on how fast the birds can fly, as loons can achieve speeds of from sixty to ninety miles per hour, but on the weather. If the spring is warm, then ice-out will be early on northern lakes and the loons will proceed north with little delay. But if it's cold, then the loons will wait on open water for the ice to break up, either along the coast before turning inland, or on large lakes and rivers.

Loons fly in loose flocks, which frequently increase in numbers as the loons begin to bunch up awaiting ice-out. They do not assume any formation, as geese do, and frequently there are great distances between individuals, from several hundred feet to a quarter of a mile. It is believed, however, that this loose flocking may benefit the loons when they fly over land by providing them with a better chance of spotting open water. When one loon sees a resting place, more distant loons will be alerted by its descent and follow.

Loons call during migration to maintain contact. In early spring you can sometimes hear them. Over land they fly quite high, often as high as fifteen hundred feet as compared with flying just a few feet off the water as they do along the coast. I remember one day in my garden, a cold, cloudy day, hearing an uncanny sound. Faintly, from a distance far above me, from within the thick ceiling of clouds that hung over Vermont, there came a loon's laughter. It was unmistakable and repeated with the quick rhythm of the bird's flight. It took me into summer. I felt for a moment like I would just go farther north with the bird and find myself in the familiar setting I associated with that laughter. But it flew on very rapidly and was gone, leaving me on my knees in the mud of early April.

Loons, during migration, do not assume the V formation common to Canada geese, or the long threadlike lines of snow geese, but fly north or south individually or in small, loose flocks of up to fifteen individuals. Often there is considerable distance between birds, and contact is maintained through calling, using the tremolo.

SPRING -
Courtship

On the northern lakes in April and early May the ice begins
to snap and groan. After the silence of winter, this is deeply
startling, like the first pecking from within an egg. One listens
closely to the egg as to the icy shell that contains the lake and
knows that another cycle is beginning, that life will go around
again — another little chick, another spring.

As the days pass, the snow over the ice melts gradually, the
ice grows porous, turns dark as it sinks a little in the water.
Winter's rigidity is relaxing. On south-facing banks the snow
begins to melt, exposing the browns and rusts of last year's dead
leaves, as if another autumn has returned. But there is an entirely different feeling in the air, not the tiredness and resignation of
autumn. The smells are fresh — of soil, newly thawed, and of
water. It is always surprising to experience the first open water.
You forget, after the stillness of a frozen world, what a fresh,
elemental smell it has and how lively it is. In the sunlight of
spring, the water sparkles in a way you never would have no-
ticed in autumn.

Ice-out — what a wonderful, stark term that conveys the
excitement yet simplicity of the time. Water — changing from
solid to liquid — this is what dominates the awareness of anyone
in the early spring who lives on a lake. You want the season to

White Trillium

move along, for the lake to hurry and thaw, the snow to melt and clear away, yet this brisk attitude of spring-cleaning is offset by an extraordinary peacefulness and languor when you feel the power that the warm sun has to accomplish the change without our help. Everything gets warmed — soil, trees, water — and with the warmth, the forest and the lake come to life.

This is when the loons return. As if the sparkle of the open water did not supply enough fascination on a warm spring day, unexpectedly, from somewhere up above, there comes the tremolo of a loon. You quickly scan the lake and the blue sky, suddenly alerted, excited, and then, over the treetops it appears — the small dark form of a rapidly flying bird. It comes into focus, the sharp white of its breast catching the sun, and you catch your breath. "The loons are back!" It is exclaimed in town to those who may not know. "The loons are back!" It is the sharing of one of the simple pleasures of country life.

✢   ✢   ✢

Once a loon has arrived on a lake, if it is going to nest, it will begin to establish its territory and defend its boundaries. Frequently the first loons to return are male. They paddle the lake with an unconscious checklist of conditions, cruising the lake, perhaps unaware of what they are looking for, yet when they do come upon an area with the right combination of features, pausing until that stretch of water begins to feel like home.

There are many requirements that determine whether or not a territory is adequate. Before lakes were so populated, it was much easier for a loon to locate an area that fulfilled them all. Now, with pressures on loon habitat increasing each year, a loon simply may not find a suitable place to nest and rear young. The success of a whole summer's efforts for a breeding pair depends largely on this initial choice.

Dog-toothed Violet

The first essential is that there be fish. This may sound obvious, but with acid rain increasingly affecting the Northeast, many lakes, which for hundreds of years have supported several pairs of loons, have now suddenly lost their fish populations. Loons may return to such a lake in the spring, return to territories they themselves have occupied for years, only to discover that there are no fish swimming below. If they can find another lake with suitable territory, they may go there to nest, but they may also abandon nesting altogether and join the ranks of loons that sit out the breeding season, simply loafing until autumn, when they will head south again.

When you think how relatively few chicks a loon produces in its lifetime compared with waterfowl such as ducks and geese, then you can appreciate the consequences of a mature pair failing to nest. A pair of mergansers, for instance, can easily produce ten ducklings in a summer. Under optimum conditions, hatching two chicks a year, it would take a pair of loons five years to hatch that many offspring. With acid rain eliminating whole lakes from potential loon use, with nesting habitats being increasingly taken over by second homes, with predators like raccoons and gulls proliferating due to an increase in food supply offered by garbage dumps — to name just a few of the obstacles loons face — it is rare that those ten chicks would all actually survive. It is just as common for a pair of loons to go year after year with no young raised.

Once a male loon has located a lake with an adequate fish population, he paddles along with several other requirements to satisfy. A loon pair, in order to raise chicks, needs quite a large territory. This might be a whole lake of from ten to two hundred acres, or an area on a larger lake defined by geographical boundaries. A loon might choose a cove, for example, and stake out all the water between a point of land to the west and an island to the east. That expanse of water would have to be large

The Common Loon once nested as far south as northern California, Iowa, Illinois, Indiana, Ohio, Pennsylvania, and Connecticut. Now, due to loss of habitat, its breeding range includes only the northern tier of the United States, and continues to include Canada, Greenland, Iceland, and Alaska, out to the tip of the Aleutian Islands.

enough to provide room for territorial and courtship displays. It would also have to be long enough for the loons to take flight and still clear the trees at the lake's edge. It must be an area large enough to provide sufficient fishing for the pair to raise their young over the entire summer. The water must be clear enough so that the loons can pursue fish to the bottom of the lake and still be able to see to catch them.

In addition, the territory must have at least one suitable nest site. Loons prefer to nest on islands and have the greatest success nesting there, island dwelling discouraging easy predation by land animals such as the raccoon. The farther an island is from shore, generally the less apt raccoons are to swim to it. However, some large islands do occasionally support resident coon populations.

Another factor that often works against loons is that islands, large or small, also frequently support resident human populations. People seek their own little domains, whether it is just for a weekend, to pitch a tent on an island, or whether it is for a lifetime and for generations to come, to build a house where one can escape the world. With loons forced to nest more frequently on the shores of the mainland, the percentage of chicks actually hatched relative to the number of nesting attempts has dropped off enormously.

Wherever the nest site, mainland or island, its orientation to the rest of the lake is also very important. It must be protected from the direct action of the waves that cross the lake in windy or stormy weather, and it must be out of the path of the general flow of boat wakes. Since loons are so inept on land, their nests are never apt to be high off the water, nor a great distance from the shoreline. A few good waves washing over a nest, particularly when the incubating bird is absent, can be fatal, either chilling the life within the eggs or actually pitching them out of the nest. A related problem, less easy for a loon to anticipate without some prior familiarity with flood control and electrical power generation, is the fluctuation of water level which frequently plagues loons nesting on a man-made lake. A pair of loons can no sooner have a nest made and their eggs laid than find themselves either high and dry, yards and yards from the water, or else, at the opposite extreme, swamped. Of course, this problem is so relatively new and unpredictable, it would be impossible for a male loon to have already acquired the instincts to avoid it.

Finally, in choosing a nest site, there is the issue of privacy. Loons will tolerate a considerable amount of company on a lake, especially when they are off the nest, but they are sensitive to disturbance when it comes to protection of their eggs and their chicks. Generally loons will be attracted to the more remote areas of a lake and to the backsides of islands. Man-made lakes with large deep-water channels to which boaters are confined in the interest of protecting their motors from striking bottom, make ideal situations, inadvertently leaving large areas of shallower water to wildlife. Unfortunately, this water is always accessible to canoeists, whose tastes for privacy and peace usually run along the same lines as those of the loon. One defense a loon has,

When the loon is being pursued by an aggressor, it runs over the surface of the water, uttering the tremolo and flapping its wings.

and which figures into its choice of a nest site, is to lay its eggs on a shore that provides a deep-water entry. This means that an approaching loon, coming to take its place on the nest, can arrive underwater and surface at just the last moment, when it is in the cover of shore. The same is true for departure. It can slide off the nest headfirst into the water and disappear, leaving animal predators and humans unaware that it is using a particular area.

✻ ✻ ✻

Not all loons go through such a complex search for appropriate territory. The male loon of an already mated pair generally returns not only to the same lake where he and his mate have nested before, but often to the same territory and even the same nest site he and his mate have used in years past.

The male arrives soon after ice-out, perhaps as much as two

weeks ahead of his mate. He splashes down, the clumsy landing of a heavy-boned bird reaching its final destination after a long and tiring flight. The surroundings are familiar after years of summering in the same cove. It could even be the cove where he himself was raised as a chick. A large boulder rises out of the water in its accustomed place, unbudged by the rigors of winter, in the exact position from which it has always reflected the late afternoon light. Two sentinel pine trees stand together on a point that marks the boundary of the loon's territory. They cast familiar shadows out over the lake. In the backwater of the cove the cattails are just emerging. A beaver is out exploring the newly open water. The lake seems peaceful, quiet, and undisturbed after all the many rivers and lakes on which the loon has stopped on his way north.

These two positions indicate that the loon is watchful, anticipating danger.

"Aaaaaaaaaahhhhhhhooooooooooooooo" — for the first time since last fall the mountains echo with the loon's ancient call. "Aaaaaahhhhhooooooooooooo." He uses the wail call to contact his mate. "Aaaaaaaaaahhhhhhhoooooooo." "Where aaaaaaarre yooouuuuu?" But there is no reply, only the distant, diminishing repetition of the same call, "Where aaaare you?" "Where aaaaaare y," "Where are y," "Where are . . . "

The days pass. The loon reclaims his old territory, and announces this boldly to other loons that splash down on the lake, making their way north, always on the lookout for nesting places. He makes known, with the wildly undulating yodel, that the cove is his. And when a male swims too close, perhaps to test the conviction of the loon, he rears up on his tail and points his bill at the intruder, flapping his wings in the water. This has been his cove for years. He and his mate have raised their chicks here successfully. It is spring and time to raise chicks again. He announces this with the yodel to all the lake. The yodels echo and repeat in the mountains, undulating even more wildly among the rocky cliffs. This cove is his. And he waits.

In territorial defense, the loon slaps the water with its feet before diving, sending up spray and making a splashing sound.

Of course, his mate may not return. She may not have survived the long winter on the ocean. She might have been pulled up with a haul of cod, entangled, and drowned in a massive fishing net, tossed back into the water or tossed into a bin for undesirable fish. She might have dived and surfaced into an oil slick left by a freighter cleaning its tanks. She might have been poisoned, perhaps wintering in the mouth of a large river, subjecting herself unknowingly to all the whims and accidents of man on a thousand tributaries upstream. The ocean is distant, immense. Who knows all that can happen over the long migrations, over the months that lie between autumn and spring.

But then, one day he hears, coming distantly, from across the lake — "Aaaaaaaaaahhhhhhhhhooooooooo." The hills are not mocking him with echoes. This call has come first and his own becomes its echo. "Aaaaaaaaaaaahhhhhhhhooooooooo."

"Aaaaaaaaaahhhhhhhhhhooooooooooo." The voice of his mate is as familiar to him as his own. She is somewhere out on the lake. He runs over the water, half flies from where he has been diving along the shore. He calls again and hears her reply, the two calls echoing and mingling among the mountains. And then she appears, flying low, uttering the tremolo, a faint laughter that trails over the lake behind her like a streamer of sound, laughing with that slight edge of anxiety that always seems to accompany even the softest tremolo in flight. Her wings move faster than sight can follow and, just as abruptly as she came into sight over the lake, she drops down and splashes into the water not far from the cove. She is back. A new year has truly begun.

No need to call now. No need to advertise their presence on the lake unnecessarily. Now they utter soft calls or kwuks, conversation between loons. He bows his head and tucks his bill to show his nonaggression; she does the same. They circle, and circle again, growing reaccustomed to one another's presence on the water, displaying their nonaggression, making it clear in the

In this posture, a courtship display, the bill is dipped in the water, sometimes rapidly, and the head often turned to the side.

2

rounded curves of their necks, in the hiding of their bills that they are not enemies, that they do not compete. In obedience to the laws of nature, they circle together, their wakes intermingling, reflecting the dark greens of the pines, the black and white of their stripes and spots, the blue of the sky. He dives beneath the surface, into the dim green other world where only her white breast and paddling feet are visible. He tests her interest in his presence. She dives to follow. He surfaces and so does she.

In this courtship display, the loon jerks its head forward and backward before the dive is actually made.

And so their courtship continues, over several days, interspersed with time spent searching the deep waters of the lake for newly emerging frogs and fish, and with time spent sleeping on the dark water at night. For days they fall into circling, into the tucking of the bill, the dives, and the circling — all symbolic of the forces working within them, drawing them together again after all these months and miles they been apart.

Then one day the female does a startling thing. She approaches the shore, nervous, anxiously circling. She doubles back and reapproaches, watching to see if the male follows. Twigs and branches protrude from the water, impeding her approach, seeming to make the land bristle. Trees rise rigidly from the ground, seeming to fix the land with their roots, seeming to tie it and prevent movement. The soil, the pebbles are so still, so inert, and so foreign to the loons. Yet the loons need the land at that moment. It is deeply ironic that one of the most perfectly adapted water birds needs the land in order to mate. The water will support the weight of ducks in the act of copulation, but the loons must trust the land. Clumsy and unaccustomed to the strange solidity, the female extends her head up over the ground and pushes herself onto shore.

A nonaggressive courtship posture, with the head held to the side and the bill down.

She looks back to see if the male follows; she seems to beckon and then moves forward herself. There in the brush, hidden among the bare twigs, is the old nest. It has been flattened by the weight of the winter's load of snow. The short trail

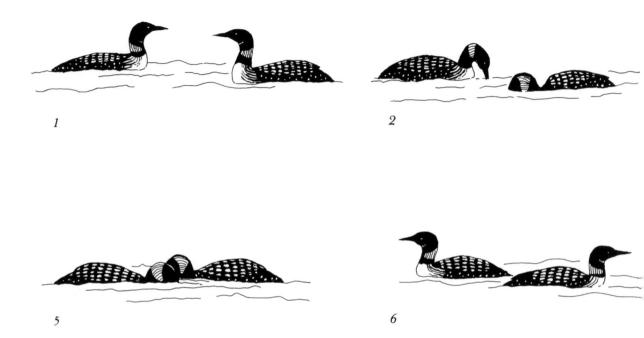

1

2

5

6

Circling is used during courtship. The loons swim in tight circles, looking in all directions.

to it, worn by countless passages of a loon's breast, is strewn with a year's accumulation of twigs and stones, but the nest is still intact, still faintly dished to hold eggs, still gently shaped to the contour of a loon's breast.

The female again looks back to see if the male follows. He does. He pushes himself up onto the shore, feeling the sudden resistance of the land. Now his feet, rather than propelling him with grace, push ineffectually sideways, working beneath the weight of his body, against moss and leaves, until he reaches her and they mate. He climbs onto her back, pauses several seconds, bowed over her, and then slides down her shoulder and into the water. This is all that is necessary to begin new life. The female

3   4

7   8

stays on the land and, in a ritualized way, still part of the dance
of courtship, pulls at twigs and dried grasses and adds them to
the nest.

   Over the next week the loons will spend a lot of time near
the nest, diving to the lake bottom, pulling up more twigs,
weaving them with moss and sedge to make a secure container
for their eggs. They repeat their courtship, bowing their heads,
dipping their bills, and come several more times to the land to
mate. It is a curious interval of time they begin with this mating,
a full month that they will take turns spending on shore, with the
willows budding out around them, the grass sprouting up alongside, and the land everlastingly still.

SUMMER-Nesting

The eggs, two of them, lie in the nest with commanding presence, their smooth oval shapes seeming to resist intrusion. They are mossy green, flecked with dark brown spots. They blend with the interior of the nest in color, but not in their smooth perfection. The moss and sedge are rough and textured, matted and damp, but the eggs are dry and self-contained. They are large, the size of goose eggs, and fascinating for their beauty and infinite potential.

Yet there is contradiction inherent in all this. The very shells that seem to resist intrusion simultaneously seem to invite it. The size of the eggs makes them conspicuous when the loons are off the nest. The contents of each egg — that tiny spark of life, that tentative formation of spine and heart, that slow organization of cells into a shape that will develop into a little bird — are extremely vulnerable, encased in such a fragile container. The eggs lie there, so precious for the future, symbolic of hope for a threatened species, but part of hard reality.

It is not long that the loons leave their eggs exposed to view. The male returns and clambers onto shore, up the short path and onto the nest. He turns the eggs before settling onto them and rearranges the vegetation in the nest around him. He faces the water, eyeing the lake suspiciously for danger, listening to the

Incubation is shared by both parents, the bird on the nest using the wail to summon its mate for exchange of duties. Incubation shifts vary from approximately half an hour to six hours, with the average being around two. The loons are on the nest 98% of the time; the most common reason for leaving the eggs unattended is territorial defense. Eggs hatch in twenty-eight to twenty-nine days after they are laid, generally one day apart.

Egg turning is done with the bill and is frequent during the first week of incubation. At nest exchange, the arriving bird may add vegetation to the nest and/or rearrange the eggs.

underbrush behind him for rustling that might indicate a predator's approach. Then he relaxes a little and settles into his time
on the nest.

The male loon is virtually indistinguishable from the female. He is technically apt to be a little larger, but for the human
observer it is usually difficult to tell one from the other. There
just always seems to be a loon on the nest, but if one were to
watch long enough, distantly, without disturbance, one could see
the loons take turns, each spending between thirty minutes and
six hours warming the eggs in pouches beneath their breasts. For
about twenty-nine days the loons will maintain the eggs at a
temperature of 100° F. For only about 2% of that time will the
eggs be left uncovered, primarily during nest exchange, with the
loons not far away.

And so the time passes. It is now the month of May, and off
in the forest the drumming of ruffed grouse can be heard. The
poplars leaf out, pale green with catkins, casting an increasingly
dense network of shadows over the nest. Following them, the
birches and maples extend their tender leaves, screening the
loons from view. In the shallows, the tadpoles hug the shoreline.
The bass, the pickerel, the pike come to spawn. It is a tentative,
delicate time of the year, a time to make one think nature is
doing all this for the first time.

Yet even in May, nature is already taking hold. All around
the lake, the plants and animals are gearing up to make the most
of the short time available for reproduction. There can be no
indolence or casualness about such a short summer season. The
cold winter returns too soon to the north woods, and most
species must complete their entire reproductive cycle within a
few months if they are going to survive.

The blackflies and mosquitoes emerge in swarms. Some-
how, one would think the loons would not be bothered, but, with
discomfort that is all too easy to imagine, they toss their heads to

Jack-in-the-Pulpit

Largemouth Bass

As a result of human presence on northern lakes, opportunistic feeders like gulls and crows have flourished, alternately feeding on garbage and on food such as loon eggs. On many lakes where gulls never used to visit, they now show up in large numbers, attracted by open dumps.

rid their eyes of the crawling and biting pests. Back in the recesses of the land, a twig occasionally cracks and through the leaves emerges the face of one of the many animals that prowl the shorelines searching for food. No problem with the deer that step delicately along, coming down to the water to drink, but there are also the skunks and weasels that part the tender grass, the minks peering into the shadows for nests left untended. And, worst of all, the raccoons have awakened from their winter sleep, have mated, and now search the lakeside, hungry and curious. Most of the people have not yet returned to the lake. The summer haunts of the raccoon — the garbage dumps, the trash cans in garages — don't yield their normal abundant fare. The people are not there to make offerings of saltines beneath the porch lights at night, laughing at the coons' antics, delighted at their boldness. Now there are too many coons, flourishing as a result of summer abundance, but at loose ends in the spareness of spring. They comb the shore, forced to rely on nature's traditional pickings, tiny hands reaching into crevices, feeling for crayfish and frogs, eyes bright, on the lookout for eggs, a perpetual threat to the loons.

The raccoons, the skunks, the minks, and the weasels are not the only animals on the lookout for loon eggs. The herring gulls have returned to the lake, wheeling and circling, perching on traditional rocks that are white with many years' guano. There is something that seems misplaced about the gulls' presence on the lake. Lured from the ocean, attracted by garbage dumps, scavenging the shoreline while they await the impending influx of humans, they seem almost too successful, too well adapted to man — especially when one of them discovers a loon nest left temporarily exposed, and swoops in to peck open an egg. One looks suspiciously at crows, too, however beautiful they might be, newly returned to the north. One wants them to think twice about helping themselves to loon eggs. One begins to side

Of all the animals that comb the lakeshore searching for unattended nests and eggs to feast on, none has proved as damaging to loon populations as the raccoon. Unafraid to raid garbage cans and dumps, and fed by lakeshore residents, raccoons have reached a state of imbalance with their natural environment, and a species like the loon, already adversely affected by human presence, has suffered. When a raccoon raids a nest, it not only eats the eggs, but roughs up the nest as well, thus leaving telltale evidence of who the marauder was. With the safety of island nest sites often no longer available, it has become necessary to hunt and trap raccoons in order to counterbalance the advantage human presence has afforded them.

Generally the loon on the nest has its head tucked in a position similar to that used when it is drifting on the water. The loon is always watchful for signs of impending danger, however, and responds generally with a raise of the head, turning it from side to side. If the threat is imminent, the loon lowers its head, ready to slide into the water and dive away from the nest.

with the loons, feeling protective of a species that exists in a more fragile balance with man.

And finally there is the arrival of people on the lake. Memorial Day weekend spells special disaster for loons. On most lakes, two to three weeks have already been invested in a pair of eggs, and time is a critical commodity in the north. All of a sudden, the calls of the hermit thrush and the veery are syncopated with human voices from shore. Hammering carries across the water as shutters are removed, docks repaired. Kids laugh and yell, excited over the new season, anxious to get into the lake, but intimidated by the cold. Boats emerge from boat houses, are freed from dry dock, and push through the water on trial runs.

All the while the loons stay near the nest, alert, watchful, cautious. They are careful to come and go from the nest unseen, approaching underwater and slipping silently into the protection of the green leaves on shore. They fish at a distance from the nest with feigned nonchalance, seemingly unconcerned by the holiday crowd. But the loons' caution is perhaps their downfall. They have kept the fact that they have a nest a perfect secret. No doubt if the people in one of the cabins up the lake, preparing a picnic and packing their boat up with gear, knew that the loons had a nest and eggs in the cove they would not be planning to spend the day there themselves. No doubt they would plan to go

During incubation, blackflies are frequently a disturbance, the loon tossing its head to be rid of them.

elsewhere, pausing at a distance to try and glimpse the loons through binoculars. But how could they know that their destination is the very shore the loons have chosen for their nest?

The female loon watches through her screen of leaves as a boat comes plowing up the lake, watches as it turns toward the cove, and listens as its motor slows and its bow settles down in the water. The loon lowers her head and neck flat to the nest, determined not to be seen, while the motor idles and the boat purrs into the cove on the momentum left from its passage across the lake. The people are excited, looking around for a good tie-up, a sunny place to spend an unseasonably pleasant day. The loon is absolutely motionless, reluctant to give up the nest, balanced, gauging what these invaders intend. The male is offshore, having approached with the boat. He gives one furtive tremolo, almost a question, expressing his sudden uncertainty. The people point to a small sandy beach, make a decision that this is the place. The kids gather up toys and lean eagerly in the direction of shore. Meanwhile the female can tolerate the boat's approach no longer. She slides off the nest, through the leaves, and dives absolutely silently. The motor is cut, the boat glides slowly to the beach, the motor is raised, and the people disembark with the day's supplies, delighted with the privacy and beauty of their chosen spot.

It surprises them that no sooner have they arrived than they are treated to a strange dance of the loons. Both loons have instantly mustered all their strategies for defense, crying the tremolo, rearing up on their tails in the penguin dance, beating their wings in the water and diving, rearing up again, calling. One of them tries to lure the boat after it, looking suddenly wounded, defenseless, crying the tremolo as it struggles up the lake. But the people do not follow. For them this helplessness is just part of the dance. The loon returns and joins its mate again, splashing, exposing the full extent of its white breast, trying to look as big and intimidating as it is possible for a loon to look to a sixteen-foot boat and five happy people. The people are lost in the magic, unable to believe the beauty of this rite of spring. The loons' cries of alarm, of desperation sound like laughter to human ears, like the essence of nature and joy and well-being. The people turn to one another and back to the loons, pointing and commenting, as if they are witnessing a meteor shower or the northern lights. They have no sense of intrusion, any more than they would feel that they intruded on the stars or the aurora borealis. How could they know? The loons speak another language, the laughing, careless-sounding tremolo. The sounds bear no resemblance to a plea. Nothing is conveyed about a nest or the eggs or the coolness of the green shadows.

The loons call and circle and then finally they give up. At some point they seem to know that too much time has passed. They've reached a cold divide between past and future. There is nothing more to be done. The eggs will stay there, hidden in the brush, so perfect in the nest, but with all the development inside them stopped, until some raccoon, ambling lazily along, has the good fortune to come upon them.

※   ※   ※

But there is time to nest again. When eggs are lost, whatever the cause, loons may renest. And sometimes, if that second clutch of eggs is lost, the loons will even nest a third time. But after this the loons give up. They seem to know, for whatever reason, be it natural selection or innate sense, that after the third week in June it is too late, that not enough time will remain for their young to learn to fly before the winter winds bear down, before the lake freezes up once more.

For over a week the loons follow the shoreline, looking for a new place to build their nest. They don't want to risk repeating the fate of the last eggs by staying in the cove. Instinct urges them to try their chances elsewhere on the lake. And so they paddle, patiently surveying, waiting for one particular location to draw them in with the right combination of conditions — deep-water approach, privacy, protection from the wave action of the lake, remoteness from human activity. This is a lot to compute, but, more than likely, there is no juggling of pros and cons. The decisions are probably made on an unconscious level. The loons just wait for the feel of a particular bit of shore to be right, to renew what we would call optimism, to begin the whole sequence of courtship, mating, and nest-building all over again.

But this is not so easy. The lake is not as remote as in years past. Improved roads have made it easily accessible, and the shorelines hide more little cabins than are at first perceived. They are sheltered in the trees, tucked around promontories, planted up on rocky points, while some of the larger camps are boldly laid out in clearings. With the beginning of June, the number of boats steadily increases, and the loons have to be watchful as they cruise the lake.

At last they center in on a new territory. It is not ideal. It has no islands. But there is a peaceful little backwater just right for the raising of chicks. The male begins to defend the territory, challenging not just other loons, but any ducks that try to cross

Common Merganser with ducklings

the water that he now looks on as his own. The pair takes up courtship once more but this time it is a little abbreviated. In mid-June, with the mergansers already trailing long lines of ducklings, there is an increased sense of urgency. Now is the time to be on the nest, not swimming the lake as a pair as if it were spring. At last the loons choose a rocky promontory in the shelter of the backwater. They again pull weeds from the bottom, weave carex and cattails, pull iris and fern, until the nest is large and strong. Then the female lays two more green eggs and the waiting begins again.

✳   ✳   ✳

After the middle of June, the human population increases at a steady rate. The schools let out. Summer camps fill up. The thumps of paddles banged against the sides of aluminum canoes carry across the water as convoys of kids explore the coves and bays. Campsites are steadily occupied, and resourceful campers clear new areas rather than be turned away to other lakes. Cabins are centers of activity all week long. Sailboats move lazily up and down the lake. Fishermen come out in the early mornings and evenings. Water-skiers speed across the water, cutting wide arcs at the ends of their towropes, and boats circle again and again to pick up skiers when they fall. June is a busy, bright time. Everyone seems to have something he wants to do.

Yet the loons watch with suspicion. They live in another world in the backwater where they nest. They are not looking for excitement. Each new form that human entertainment takes seems to pose a new threat. The sounds of the motors, the banging of the paddles, the voices reach the backwater as a cacophony of isolated sounds, each to be evaluated for its potential danger. The canoeists slipping peacefully along the shorelines seem to move with stealth. The fishermen who anchor and settle into sensing the minute action of nibbles at the ends of their lines, talking softly among themselves in the twilight or silently enjoying their nonverbal telepathy with the underwater life of the lake, seem threatening by virtue of their very stillness. They wiggle their boats into remote corners and stay there instead of speeding on like other boats. The water-skiers, careening along, seem dangerously mobile, skittery, unpredictable, their weaving back and forth increasing the reach of their boats' swaths down the lake. The loons are outsiders to the fun, taking turns on the nest, watching uneasily, raising their heads up for a better view or lowering them down to hide.

June passes safely, but next comes the Fourth of July. It is just a chance occurrence of our calendar, some mismatch of our needs and loons', that Memorial Day and the Fourth of July fall when they do. A pair of loons that loses a clutch of eggs in the frenzy of the Memorial Day weekend will frequently lay new eggs approximately ten days to two weeks later, or about June twelfth. Thus, by the weekend of the Fourth of July, when extra-large crowds of vacationers again converge on the lakes, these new eggs will have been incubated approximately twenty-two days, just a week short of the twenty-nine necessary to fully form the embryos. Thus, the same sort of frustrating situation can occur for the same pair of loons twice in one summer — eggs laid in the middle of May lost on the thirtieth, and eggs laid in the middle of June lost on the Fourth of July. The timing couldn't be

Great Blue Herons

worse. So much time may be expended in each of the two unsuccessful nestings that a third attempt is out of the question. This might seem like a fairly inconsequential situation, an exceptional circumstance rather than a rule, yet more and more it is being realized that these two weekends and their timing play particular havoc with nesting success. After the Fourth, a considerable number of loons are seen idling away the rest of the summer, flocking up with other loons that also don't have chicks.

The backwater proves to be sufficiently protected, however, so that this weekend, too, comes and goes and the eggs are safe. The lake returns to its normal level of activity. The summer solstice is just past and the days are long and warm. What a difference there is between this setting and the very simplified scene of the winter solstice when the loons were on the ocean. Now there is abundance and variety everywhere. Overhead the sun is hot, causing the loon on the nest to lie flat and pant to stay cool. In the blue sky gulls glide, kingfishers dart from lookout to lookout, herons unexpectedly bark like dogs, flying slowly overhead, alone or in pairs.

Baby Skunks

The green of the land is at its height, each leaf full-size, as green as it will ever be. Most of the woodland animals have given birth, and now, instead of solitary skunks, there is a line of them, black and white, making their way through the leaves. The foxes have pups, tumbling and exploring. The coons are followed by an inquisitive brood of pointy-faced little masked duplicates, all of them eagerly poking and searching for food. Now the lightning bugs have begun to twinkle along the shoreline at dusk, edging the lake with stars. In thunderstorms they seem to blink faster, fearlessly beckoning the lightning bolts to earth, secure beneath the giant old pines. On clear nights they seem to blink to the stars, abundant in the northern clarity, and to the cool, white moon moving slowly through its phases, passing slowly through the month.

Beneath the loons, in the damp, dark world of the nest, the eggs, too, pass smoothly from phase to phase, golden yolks gradually giving way to the darkness of black down. It will not be long now. The loons take their turns on the nest, waiting out the long, hot days, waiting out the dark night, calling, "Aaaahhh-hooooo." "Where are you? The land is tiring in its stillness. Come take your turn on the nest."

Water Lily

SUMMER-
Chicks

In the moonlight of a warm night in mid-July, the male loon, which is on the nest, stretches his neck forward, opens his bill slightly, and calls the long wail to his mate. He calls again, in quick succession, leaving her no time to reply. The granite mountains bounce the calls off rock faces, and through the darkness the female loon approaches over the water.

In the nest, within one of the downy pouches where he warms the eggs, the male has felt the smallest movement — hardly there, but undeniable. It is the first pecking.

He calls again. The calls resound in the mountains, but his mate is already nearby, cutting a V across the glassy surface of the water.

They speak in soft tones, kwukking. She dunks her head instinctively, lifts up and stretches her wings. There is the sense that something is to be done, but there is nothing to do but wait.

Again the pecking . . . an insistent, dull tapping from within one of the eggs, a complaint against the dark incurving walls of the shell that limits space. Peck . . . tap . . . peck . . . from out of the stillness of twenty-nine days there suddenly arises urgency, a need for room. The little chick needs to stretch its neck out straight, needs to extend its tiny wings, needs to uncurl its little legs. It is ready to join this world of moonlight and stars, this

Blue Flag Iris

world of lake water and breezes and blue sky and trees. It needs to breathe. The big loon hoists himself to one side on the nest, and there, from a small hole on the side of one of the eggs, protrudes a tiny beak.

More struggle, more pecking . . . and resting and pecking. . . . It is so much work for little muscles being used for the first time. Peck . . . rest . . . peck . . . and then finally a side of the shell falls away and there, wet and tired and wavering, is a very small black chick with a little white breast.

The father loon kwuks softly, expressing the bond between himself and this new bit of life before him in the nest. His mate hears the gentle tone and knows there is a chick. But the little chick, for that night, will know nothing more than the warmth to be found beneath a loon's breast.

In the morning the second egg still has not hatched. At

dawn the female loon is on the nest. The little chick that emerged from the shell the night before pokes his head up and out through her wing . . . daylight! The sunshine is reflected on the water and dances before his eyes. All the world is light and air and movement.

The chick pushes forward, slides down the speckled side of the big loon and back into the nest . . . curiosity. Little bits of sand and grass . . . peck . . . peck . . . peck . . . his little beak works almost without his knowing it as he makes his way over the sticks. This is his first food, these little bits of weed, and the grit lodges in his gizzard to digest it.

He spends the morning like this, pecking, poking around the nest, alternately retreating to the shelter of the loon's wings or climbing up on her back to absorb the hot sun. His down is dry and fluffy and his mother preens it with her own oil to make him ready for the water.

By afternoon he has had enough of the nest. He has pecked over it all. He has tasted the sedge, the moss, the willow; he has nibbled up all the bits of dirt and sand he can use. He has gone under, up and around, back and through his mother's wings. He has napped. He has preened. He has stretched his wings.

Now there is that water down there. He has felt his parents' breasts damp with it when they climb on the nest. The way it glitters attracts him, the way it weaves and wanders with reflections of the sky and the overhanging hemlocks. He has seen his parents come and go from it, floating smoothly over its surface. Now is the time for him to venture down the side of the nest.

The reeds and sticks are uneven. He teeters, peeping, and his father, in the water, calls softly in return. Little waves, hardly ripples, come to meet him at the water's edge. He peeps, his father answers, he pauses for a moment and then pushes his tiny breast onto the surface of the water. It holds him, and his feet paddle instinctively, pushing him away from land. It will likely be

Loons have precocial young. This means that the chicks are born already covered with down. They are able to maneuver around the nest on the first day after they are hatched, finding their own grit and bits of vegetation. They are also able to swim within a day, needing only to have their down oiled by an adult before they enter the water. To understand the advantages of a precocial chick, picture an altricial bird like the robin. Born bare-skinned and vulnerable, it is totally dependent on its parents for its care.

three to four years before he touches land again, but his father is there ahead, big, familiar, someone to be followed.

The female loon remains on the nest. Generally the eggs hatch about a day apart, so she waits. The sun passes overhead and, just before dusk, a new little head pokes out from beneath her wing. Peep . . . peep . . . the chick wiggles free, climbs up on her back to rest.

So there will be two chicks to raise this year. The loons have done well. Other pairs will not be so lucky. On many lakes the average hatch for a pair of loons is .50 — that is, one half chick per year or one whole chick every two years. On some wilderness lakes the average is high — .93 in northern Minnesota, for example — but on other lakes it is disastrously worse. On New Hampshire's largest lake, Lake Winnipesaukee, with an area of 44,586 acres, there were sixty to seventy adult loons sighted in the summer of 1956. Just two decades later, in 1976, there were only fifteen sighted. From those fifteen, only one chick was actually hatched. In more recent summers, the situation has improved slightly due to the use of artificial nesting platforms and careful tending of young chicks and their parents by concerned officials, but residents of the lake struggle to increase a loon population that was shockingly diminished before people took note, and there is always the sense of working against tremendous odds.

To have two chicks, then, is very lucky, more like the old days, when to see a pair of loons with a chick riding on the back of each adult was common. Yet success is not assured just because the eggs have both hatched. While life gets increasingly safer as a chick matures, there is a whole summer ahead, and the

The artificial nesting platform is a man-made device, built of cedar posts and wire mesh, covered with sod and indigenous vegetation, and anchored with cement blocks. Given its ability to rise and fall with fluctuating water levels, this floating island has become a vital tool in preserving the loon.

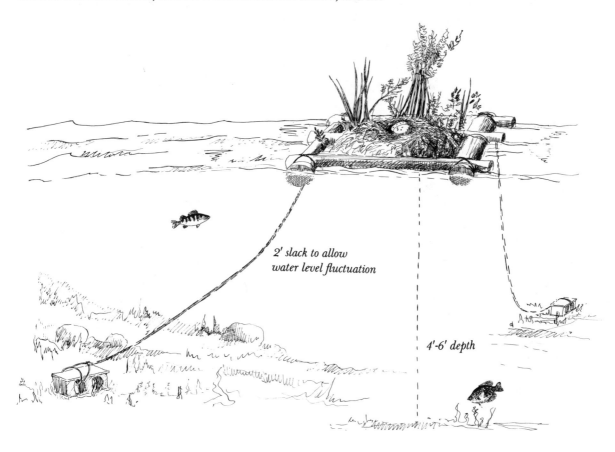

2' slack to allow water level fluctuation

4'-6' depth

chicks are very tiny and vulnerable, with much to learn.

In the morning the female loon is again on the nest. She and the male have taken turns over the night tending the two chicks, the one still in the nest and the other in the water. Now, with the dawn, with both chicks hatched, she is ready to leave the land. For two months she has needed its solidity, she has been drawn to it as a place to hold her eggs, to keep them dry. But now that need is gone. Now the water invites her to rejoin it and leave the shore for another year.

She slides down the side of the nest. It is nearly dawn. No people are on the lake. The water is glassy beneath a misty low fog. She enters the water without a sound, glides a moment through the fog, and turns. High and dry on the nest the little chick looks surprised. Who is coming back to protect him? He waits for one parent or the other to rejoin him on the nest but neither does. They are through with the land. A door has been silently shut on that phase of the year. Now it is truly summer and time to have two chicks on the water.

The parents call and beckon softly, urging the chick from land. Water is where a loon belongs. They urge it to come join its brother — two little male loons this year. The adults are anxious to be gone, to retreat deeper into the backwater, to slip their chicks out of sight until they are bigger and stronger. They beckon, and at last the chick starts to move, up out of the bowl of the nest, down over the side, peeping, looking to his parents. Momentarily the water reflects his tiny form before he lays his breast trustingly on it and floats.

How vast the water is! The chicks cannot see the end of it. They look across the lake's surface, past wave after wave, and there is only more water. They lower their heads beneath the surface and peer just like their parents, and find they are suspended above a totally different realm, yellow-green near the surface, but deepening into a dark and bottomless world they

Once chicks are hatched and in the water, they still are not out of danger from predators. Besides gulls, which can swoop down and attack a chick, from below there is the danger of large turtles or fish reaching up and snagging a bite-size little bird.

don't dare to explore.

Their parents keep watch in both hemispheres, scanning the sky that arcs overhead and frequently peering beneath the surface of the lake. The little chicks weigh only a few ounces, easy bitefuls for predators on all sides. Wheeling above, the ever-present gulls have a good vantage point from which to notice any chicks or ducklings left unguarded. In a moment they could be down to drown and eat a loon chick. Beneath the surface the great ancient snapping turtles have a fondness for tiny birds. They slip through the depths like mossy dragons, peering upward toward the light, waiting to chance upon the silhouettes of

chicks or ducklings with their convenient dangling feet. The same is true of the huge pike and bass that survive in the depths. The white undersides of the chicks, which from some angles blend with the bright light of the surface, are inadequate defense against these monsters that watch keenly from below.

As they head off deeper into the privacy of the backwater, the chicks weave back and forth between their parents, zigzagging, imprinting the appearance of each adult, learning to stay close. It is a long trip for three ounces of muscle and fluff so newly hatched. The weaving and zigzagging make the trip twice as long. The parents go slowly, but before long they stop and offer the chicks rides.

It is easy to understand the relief of a little chick allowed to ride on its parent's back. Not only does back-riding offer protection from predators, but the chick's down is easily soaked after a relatively short time in the water, and being elevated onto the warm back of an adult loon gives it the chance to dry. In the first two weeks, a chick is apt to ride as much as 65% of the time. The parent swims alongside, submerges low enough for the chick to scramble on, and then rises and lifts it clear of the water. The chick settles either under one of the adult's wings, facing front, or up on top of the back facing either direction, its little feet tucked under its own warm belly. This arrangement takes the place of going to land to rest and get warm, as one frequently sees a group of merganser ducklings do, occupying a sunny, flat rock for an hour or two.

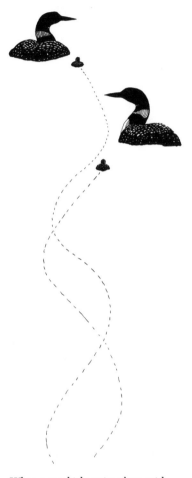

When new chicks swim along with the adult loons, they often zigzag back and forth between the two, imprinting the appearance of each adult in their memories and staying safely nearby.

　　　*　　　　*　　　　*

The backwater is protected from much of the human activity on the lake by the shallowness at its entrance. To enter its more remote coves, the loons navigate a maze of promontories from which cattails and willows grow, screening the inner

Back-riding is of considerable importance for loon chicks. In the first two weeks, it may well occupy 65% of their time. Two chicks may ride on one parent or one chick may be on the back of each. Back-riding not only offers safety from predators, particularly large fish and snapping turtles, but is also a means of brooding. Under the wing of the adult, feathers are sparse and, therefore, the chick makes direct contact with warm skin. In addition, the chick is lifted out of the chilly water, where its down could eventually become soaked, and up onto a black surface where the chick's own black down can absorb the sun. Since loons rarely return to the nest once their young are hatched, back-riding provides an effective substitute.

reaches of the water from the view of boaters. The reflections of the trees that line the shore are clear and brilliant on water so little disturbed by wind and waves, and yellow water lilies dot the surface among glossy dark lily pads that lie flat and still. This is the secret domain of the moose, who come to wade in the shallows, to eat the lily roots and escape the biting flies in the woods. It is the fishing grounds of the great blue herons, who stalk the shallows on pencil-thin legs. It is the home of beavers, who seldom have need to slap their tails, but patrol between lodges undisturbed, their noses cutting wakes that widen behind them across the still water. And for the next several weeks it will be the nursery of the loons, a quiet place where the chicks can learn their first lessons, practice new skills, and have a chance to grow and strengthen their muscles before contending with the dangers of the open lake.

For the first eight weeks the chicks are dependent on their parents to bring them food. Often, when the chicks are floating on the surface, peering below, they will see one of their parents jet past and disappear out of sight into the depths of the lake. The chicks wait and, when the adult reemerges, they swim over, peeping. The big loon may hold a small crayfish in its bill, a snail, a frog, or a salamander or any of a number of aquatic insects, or it may have caught a minnow or the fry of some larger fish. Though it may have already killed the food, especially to give it to very small chicks, the adult will frequently splash it in the water as if to make it seem alive. This splashing starts the chicks begging, pecking at the base of the parent's bill until one of them is offered the food, which it swallows whole.

Though they rely on their parents to bring them food, from the very first day the chicks have the instinct to try to fish for themselves. At first this is very comical. The newly hatched chicks are so buoyant that they can scarcely submerge, and, like dry little corks, no sooner do they go under than they bob back up again. For the next few days they practice diving in the well-lit safety of shallow water, going after little strands of lake weed that swim along like green fish, not suspecting that they are

about to be devoured by a tiny black loon. As the chicks' diving ability increases, they practice streaking to the bottom like their parents, and snatching up tiny pebbles before they can escape. But it is the minnows, which taunt the chicks with their quick, flashy turns, that are the real sources of fascination. The chicks dive, propelling themselves boldly into the schools of glimmering fish, only to run out of air just as the minnows are within reach. They surface, rest a moment, and dive again, but for the first few days the minnows elude them.

At least one of their parents is with the chicks at all times, guarding them while they dive and bob, kwukking to them when they stray too far. The backwater is peaceful, with no one aware that this loon family is even on the lake. Occasionally the sound of a particularly loud boat filters back through the cattails, causing the loons to lift their heads and look, and putting the moose on guard to retreat back into the woods. Sometimes gulls take up soaring just overhead, and the loons move a little closer to their chicks to make sure their presence is known. Periodically planes

Moose

appear out of nowhere, swooping over the lake with terrifying noise and speed, causing the loon chicks to hunch on the water, their heads low, to escape detection.

Then, early one morning, a canoe enters the backwater. At first the loons are only aware of a faint sound that could have been nothing more than a beaver shifting a poplar branch or a muskrat entering the water. It is just a faint disturbance of the water, a slight rippling noise. The loons swim over to investigate, with one eye on the chicks to make sure they will stay in the cover of the shore, and there, just turning in to explore the recesses of the backwater, is a red canoe in which sit two people. They are obviously captivated by the stillness and the beauty. They feather their paddles and drift for long expanses. They make their way past the cattails like a floating log, with none of the noise that accompanies an increased desire for speed. They move in phase with the morning and with the drift of the water.

"Shhh. Loons," one of them breathes.

In slow motion they put their paddles in the canoe and drop their hands and watch.

The loons call out, the tremolo at first, seemingly reluctant to break the silence, to engage in confrontation. The canoe continues to drift in the direction of the chicks. The male calls again, the tremolo first, followed by the increased aggression of the yodel.

The loons grow increasingly uneasy. The chicks shouldn't be alone. It is just at this age that they are most easily lost. The chicks have heard their parents' calls and snuggle tighter into the shadow of a log, a shadow any fisherman would be happy to throw his line into hoping for a big fish.

The canoe continues to drift, and the loons rear up and begin to rush in its direction. They dance the penguin dance. They splash and dive. Again the male utters the yodel, sending wild undulations into the mountains. The water has lost the

glassiness of morning and now reflects the struggle of the day. The chicks, tucked into the darkness, are cold but unmoving. They hear their parents being forced deeper into the backwater, getting closer all the time.

Then all at once the male loon dives under the water and reemerges on the other side of the canoe. The loons are going to try a new trick. The female quietly dives and heads back to where they left the chicks, while the male resumes his dancing and calling on the other side of the canoe, the spectacular display which the people now have to turn their heads to see. The person in the stern slowly lifts a paddle and silently pivots the canoe. Then he paddles delicately, following the loon.

And so the canoe is led out of the backwater and into the lake. Meanwhile, the female, in a series of long dives, reaches the chicks. They have not moved. She kwuks to them and two little black forms separate from the shadow where she left them. They are chilled, actually shivering, but she submerges and lifts them both on her back and ferries them out into the warmth of the sun.

Life settles back down for the adult loons and they resume the task of providing food for the growing chicks. The chicks continue to practice their diving, pursuing fish after fish until, during their second week, they begin to surprise themselves and occasionally surface with their prey. While at two days of age they could dive only a foot in depth and cover only two feet underwater, at a week they can dive to a depth of ten feet and travel a distance of forty to sixty feet before they reemerge. By two weeks they can make a quick series of dives covering twenty to thirty yards at a time.

The chicks grow surprisingly fast. By the time they are two weeks old they are almost half the size of their parents. They are still vulnerable to predation, so they continue to be allowed to ride on their parents' backs, but it is a little amazing how quickly

Purple-flowering Raspberry

they have gone from tidy little bundles to rather awkward cargo.

The month of July comes to an end. In the backwater, the fish have begun to grow sparse, wary, temporarily depleted by the family of loons, and one foggy morning the parents head out for the open lake. The chicks are old enough now to manage the rough water, the exposure to humans, the longer distances. They dive well enough to take advantage of the better fishing. It is time to teach them the lessons of the open lake, the larger world. Summer is passing. The icy winds of autumn will have no patience with chicks unready to fend for themselves.

The lake is quiet in the early morning. The water is calm. The loons head south along the shore, spread out, and begin to dive. The chicks at first have trouble catching anything. The lake is deep and they are unaccustomed to having to go so far to reach the bottom. But the adults return with fish for them. The feeding pattern has changed somewhat now that the chicks are older. Instead of killing the prey, the big loons often just maim it and turn it loose in the water near the chicks. This gives the young loons the advantage they need, and they retrieve the food with confidence.

They spend the morning like this, staying in relatively close proximity to one another, one loon diving, then another, no loons visible, then one surfacing, and another appearing some distance away. They keep an eye on each other as they work slowly down the lake.

They are quite a distance from the backwater when the first boat of the morning is heard from up the lake. At first the sound is distant enough not to be too alarming. It is the same droning that the chicks have heard before, and they keep on diving. But the adults are alert. They stay on the surface watching. At last it can be seen, a small, dark grey silhouette on the paler grey water. It takes a while to approach. In the quiet of the morning its sound has long preceded it. Beneath the surface, the chicks hear the strange buzzing of the motor, growing steadily louder, and they surface and watch. One adult gives a tiny tremolo, a fleeting, quiet signal to the chicks to be ready. But the boat comes into full view and glides by with a steady roar, even altering its course a little to give the loons plenty of room. This is how it is on the lake. Most of the people give the loons room. They watch for them, accommodate them.

Most people — but there are a few who still look on them as some sort of black and white duck, of which there must be plenty. A couple of days after the loons have come out from the backwater, when they have begun to grow reaccustomed to the busy life of the lake, and have settled into a pattern of fishing by day and sleeping in the center of the lake at night, they are out fishing in the afternoon not far from shore. The wind has picked up. The water is quite rough. The female has just caught a bullhead and is working at avoiding its spiny fins, swimming over to offer it to one of the chicks, when a boat towing a skier suddenly appears from downwind. The loons have not heard it till it is quite close. The female calls the tremolo loudly, alerting the chicks. The chicks dive as the boat comes gliding in. The adults rear up, beating their wings. The skier arcs out, aiming straight for the male. The loon dives at the last moment, and the

Bullhead

skier passes overhead. The boat circles and the female takes off up the lake, calling the tremolo, luring the boat to follow away from her chicks. She splashes the water as visibly as possible, calling, trying to look helpless, trying to appear unable to fly. She beats a path up the lake, and the boat obediently follows. The people holler out, whooping and having fun, not feeling particularly malicious, but for the loon this is an exhausting and desperate game.

When she returns down the lake, flying, having lost the boat, the chicks are nowhere to be found. The male is near the shore, and together the two adults begin to comb the shadows. Up and down the shoreline they work, searching the cool green reflections of the maples and the pines. But the chicks do not appear. The loons kwuk to the rocks and the fallen logs but get no answer. When they reach a point of land beyond which the lakeshore turns radically, making it unlikely that the chicks would be found there, the adults double back and work up the same length of shore they have just come down. They are beginning to get frantic. There is nowhere else the chicks would have gone but to this shore. It is part of an ancient code. When there is danger, if a parent cannot take them, the chicks go alone to the nearest shore and hide. They are too big to have been swallowed by fish or turtles, but perhaps they were attacked by a

gull. Perhaps they were drowned by the boat.

The loons continue swimming up and down, searching inlets and coves, and then, as the female peers into the mottled reflections of some poplar branches in the shadow of the roots of a huge old pine, she sees them. They are staring right at her from their hideout, and when she kwuks they come out immediately. This is as it should be. It is part of the same ancient code that sent them there that has prevented their coming out again. It is not their decision. They must wait until a parent is right in front of them assuring them it is safe, even if this means letting that parent pass back and forth numerous times before the chicks are finally found.

The days pass peacefully for the loons. Boats move up and down the lake continually as people take advantage of the warm weather, but the loons have taken to fishing in an area a little removed from the main traffic. It is on the edge of their territory, round the peninsula from the backwater. The chicks grow rapidly and pass the midsummer days unaware that by their very survival they are part of a precarious minority.

AUTUMN -
Chicks maturing

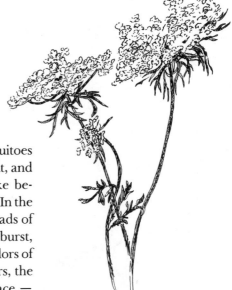

Queen Anne's Lace

August in the north is a pleasant month. The mosquitoes and blackflies have subsided, the days are clear and brilliant, and the band of trees and mountains that surrounds the lake between water and sky divides wide expanses of purest blue. In the clearings, berries have swollen to capacity and the seed heads of the flowers of spring and early summer have formed and burst, scattering wide the beginnings of another year. Now the colors of late summer flowers — the pale lavender of the wild asters, the yellow of the goldenrod, the white of the Queen Anne's lace — shimmer together, increasing the effect of the sun's brilliance. The summer has peaked. The work of regeneration seems mostly accomplished, and now there is an easy, carefree atmosphere in the air.

Yet amid this fullness and expansion, despite the sounds of laughter, splashing, and diving around the lake, there are people wise to the shape of summer, who know it does not last forever. As children they were caught off guard by the year's sudden decline into autumn, and they are already bracing themselves, changing their expectations, taking out their winter minds in advance of spotting leaves prematurely red and fallen. They do not intend to be caught again, to feel that confusion of season, that vague heaviness of heart that one feels on certain days at the apex of the year when time starts to teeter, when the green of the woods suddenly looks dull, and life seems to go out of summer. They choose to jump ahead, to adopt brisk, energetic fall attitudes, accepting right away the fact that soon the earth and all its creatures will be bargaining with winter.

To some extent, a little of this feeling may be true for the adult loons as well. As the days in August pass, the adults grow increasingly independent of their young. They have made the migration before. Perhaps the first feeling of autumn in the air brings associations with other years, creates just the first twinges of restlessness, the first awareness, however unconscious, of that whole lay of the earth beyond the surrounding mountains.

Yet the young loons are far from ready to migrate. Never mind that other loons have begun to arrive on the lake, loons whose young have already flown, or loons that for one reason or another had no chicks to raise this year. Never mind that these

loons are already beginning to flock, to gather together in antici-
pation of migration, and that the crows, too, are flocking up,
calling indecipherable directions to one another over the treetops. Never mind that in the bushes around the lake the crickets
have begun to fire up that vibrating and equally indecipherable
communication that makes hot afternoons have that slightly
dangerous sound that is a sign of summer's end. The young
loons are not ready for independence. The nest losses in the
spring, the fact that the eggs did not hatch until mid-July, have
put them behind. They still have growing to do, and much to
learn before they can hope to successfully complete the long
migration to the sea.

The third week in August the young loons are just four
weeks old. They have entered a phase comparable to adoles-
cence in humans. They can no longer be called chicks, but now
are large greyish birds that look quite out of place behind their
precisely speckled parents. They are now two-thirds the size of
adults, weighing as much as five pounds. In place of their black
down a secondary greyish down has grown in, and interspersed
with that are emerging the true feathers of their grey juvenile
plumage. Their bodies and necks have lengthened, giving them

the silhouettes of adult birds.

Yet, just as human adolescents often appear quite grown-up physically even though they may still be very immature, so the size of the young loons is misleading. There is a quality of suspension to their existence now, a neither here nor there, this nor that quality. They swim over to try and ride on their parents' backs, but when one succeeds it is so big that it virtually swamps the adult and is promptly shed back into the water. The young loons are still very dependent on their parents for food. Though their fishing ability is steadily improving, when one of the adults surfaces with a fish they still swim over begging, peeping like chicks one moment and uttering "heeuur" sounds the next. The adults leave their offspring alone more frequently now, often going off across the lake for whole days at a time, reappearing only at sunset. While they are gone, the young loons spend their time diving, fishing, acquiring the skills for survival. Yet time goes on, and one of the most important skills of all, that of flying, is still well beyond their capability. It will be another month before their primaries are fully grown and nearly a month after that before they will have learned to fly. Meanwhile, the month of August will come to an end and the month of September, with all the many changes it brings to the north, will begin with the dawn of a chilly morning.

❖ ❖ ❖

All summer the lake has seemed to belong to people. The loons have occupied the fringes, maneuvered among the boats, diving, always watching, always moving with precision, whether it is to disappear abruptly or to swim in a seemingly casual way out of the path of confrontation. Yet with each year the loons get to know the human race just a little bit better. This summer they have ventured with slightly more trust to cut closer to the ends of

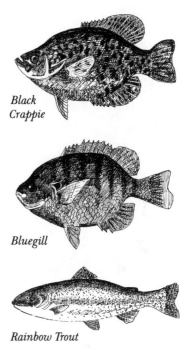

Black Crappie

Bluegill

Rainbow Trout

While loons do prey on some game fish as well as so-called trash fish, it is believed that, in general, the presence of loons on a lake may be beneficial to the game fish population, in that loons may thin out the competition from less desirable varieties. Among the fish that loons commonly eat are: bluegill, minnows, perch, smelt, trout, bass, crappies, pike, and bullheads. In addition loons eat crayfish, snails, leeches, frogs, salamanders, various insects, and aquatic plants.

docks. In the early morning, when their pursuit of fish has carried them down the lake into the thick of human habitation, they have seemed unaware of people here and there on the shore, people still sleepy, out at dawn making their first observations of the lake for the day, cupping mugs of coffee or tea, staring silently as the loons and the sun simultaneously penetrate the fog. They seem to have realized people often can be relied upon to do nothing, to just stand or sit hushed in peaceful observation. It is part of a slow change in both loons and humans, a slow withdrawal through time from former eras of callous slaughter.

With the end of the Labor Day weekend, the lake returns to the loons. Those people who remain are busy boarding up camps, securing boats, or off at work all day. The water of the lake is now disturbed by little more than breezes. It is an abrupt change. Suddenly silence is dominant. The children, who have shared the underwater domain with the loons, who have lived like fish for days or weeks or months at a time, are now dispersed into distant cities, trying to get accustomed to the feel of shoes, looking at their teachers, the four walls, and their tanned schoolmates, and wondering how they were so quickly beached and subdued. People are back to being segregated with people and whole tracts of wilderness are returned to other creatures.

Now that people have gone from the lake, the deer leave the cover of the deep woods and venture down to the shore for drinks, their feet patterning the sandy beaches with delicate Vs. The moose frequent new shallows that they haven't dared visit all summer. In the backwaters, beavers are hard at work, ranging through the woods looking for new poplar stands, felling the trees, hauling the branches back to their lodges, and securing them underwater for their winter food. Out on the open lake, the young gulls try their wings, the young ducks practice taking off and landing.

White-tailed Deer

But the juvenile loons remain earthbound, confined to the lake by gravity. They paddle about their old territory, now swimming out into the lake rather than hiding near shore when danger threatens, practicing that unique form of escape open to loons and grebes called "sinking." When a loon "sinks," it lowers its body straight down into the water like a submarine, without any of the kicking or bobbing necessary for a dive. The loon can completely disappear without a ripple, or it can merely sink to a lower level in the water, leaving just its head out like a periscope to retain sight of the danger. The way in which a loon is able to accomplish this clever means of escape is by compressing air from its feathers, lungs, and internal air sacs. Once this is done its heavy bones, which give it nearly the specific gravity of water, cause it to sink beneath the surface and out of sight.

As the month of September passes, the true nature of the deciduous trees — maples, alders, birches, ash — suddenly becomes striking. The hemlocks, the spruces, the pines face winter steadily, autumn having little effect on their deep and stoic green. Their conical shapes seem to root them all the more firmly to the earth as they stand contracted, braced, and ready for snow. But the broad-leafed trees seem one by one to throw up their hands in excitement. It is as if they had warm-blooded souls, set to flee to warmer regions, leaving only the grey bones of the trees to be weathered in the cold.

By mid-September there is actually a frost. Overnight it

An unusual form of escape that loons perform is called "sinking." By compressing air from inside its body, a loon is able to descend slowly, much like a submarine. This allows the bird to disappear without the splashing sound or ripples that might result from a dive. Also, the loon may just partially submerge to any level, so that it can avoid being seen, yet still have its eyes above the water to watch the source of danger.

turns the bracken brown and leaves the tenderer plants looking limp and bruised. It is the death blow summer seems to have been expecting. It is the first sign of winter as an active force. On the surface of the lake the young loons pass yellow, orange, red leaves, the forerunners of the millions to come.

But a few leaves are not all that is newly afloat on the water. If you could look closely just after dawn on calm mornings, you would find loon feathers floating there, too. And if you looked closely at the adult loons, you could see grey starting to invade their crisp blackness, first near the bill and then spreading down the neck, like fog coming in on a clear night, like the ocean's gradual influence on their awareness. They will not wait much longer on the lake. The impending migration's spell is in the air.

At nine weeks of age the young loons have already acquired the same tones of grey and brown that the adults will wear before leaving the summer range. Juvenile plumage complete, the young loons are nearly full grown, slightly smaller than the adults, with flight feathers that are long and straight. Now it is time for their parents to take them out in the middle of the lake and begin preparing them for flight.

But it is not easy lifting the full-size body of a loon into the air. In contrast to soaring birds, such as vultures, whose large wings permit them to wheel slowly across the sky but who are unable to fly rapidly because of the drag created by large wings, loons are designed for high speed. Their wings are small, relative to their body size, and produce little drag, allowing the birds to make long migrations at top speed, anywhere from sixty to ninety miles per hour. Yet for anything but direct flight, small wings on a large body with solid bones spell trouble. While most birds can ascend rapidly and with ease, soar through the air, and alight with precision, loons often need up to a quarter of a mile of open water over which to run, flapping their wings with stupendous effort, before their feet are finally drawn out of the

At the age of from four to six weeks, young loons begin to acquire their juvenile plumage. This consists of grey feathers that emerge among their dark greyish down, which in turn has replaced the black down that covers chicks at hatching. Thus, chicks, as they grow larger, also grow steadily lighter in color until, between their eighth and tenth week, their juvenile plumage is completely grown and the young birds are shades of pale to medium grey, brown, and white. It will not be until the juvenile loons' fourth year that they will acquire the black and white breeding plumage that so typifies loons.

water. Soaring is an impossibility, a loon's weight requiring it to flap its wings constantly; alighting amounts to a near crash landing and is only safe into water.

So the parents work at developing the wing strength and the coordination of their young, though perhaps not deliberately. Whether they engage them in races just for fun or out of a sense of competition or as a result of natural selection, those loons survive over the years whose parents have prepared them well for flight, and they in turn prepare offspring of their own. Who knows what level of concern motivates an animal in the care of its young? Nonetheless, the adults seem to drill their young with races up and down the lake. As the days of practice pass, the juvenile loons' speed and stamina increase. They swim out into open water and, seeing one of their parents running over the surface, they join in, just as if they already knew how to fly, beating their wings, thrashing the water and drawing Vs out behind, which lengthen and widen steadily and serenely in contrast with the loons' agitation. But, as abruptly as the race begins, it ends. The parent takes flight heavily, with little ease, but the breasts of the young loons slip back into the water. Their body weight still exceeds their strength and experience; it will not be lifted from the water on such little-tried wings. The cooling lake, crossed by the wakes of other birds arriving and leaving en route, littered with an increasing collection of leaves, remains their only domain. They swim idly for a while and then turn and race back up the lake, preoccupied, as youth always is, with the next challenge to its development.

Then one day, as if by accident, one of the young loons flies. It has sped down the lake with its parents and its sibling, and they have all come to a stop one by one, resigning their breasts back to the water. Then they have raced back again, splashing, calling, lacking all shyness, as if making up to themselves for the time that motorboats dominated the same space. Then back

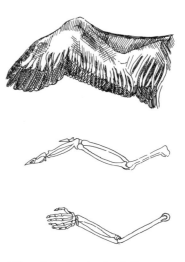

Although the loon's wing is far removed in structure from the forelimbs of primitive reptiles, from which it evolved, a look at the illustration of Archaeopteryx *(page 124) gives one an idea of just how the wing developed. Comparison with the human forearm is interesting because it shows how the bird has been specifically adapted for flight.*

again — down lake, all of them, four loons making a display of the reserve energy of the species. Only, instead of four of them stopping and racing back again, one of the juveniles feels its body start to lift, the air cool its feet, and it rises clear of the water. Flight is not without effort, but it must be a surprise to see the water start to recede below, to feel the air all around, to see the tall hemlocks drop steadily away within a pattern of dark green and flame. It must be unnerving to see the lake, always constant and all-encompassing before, flatten out below — separate, shimmering, merely a shape determined by the hills that hold it — and to see other lakes appear, silver and level in the pockets between the mountains.

The young loon circles, wings working with tremendous exertion, automatically making the necessary changes in angle to accomplish a return. He can see the other loons, far below, stopped now, no longer racing. He can tell their shape and size from the air by instinct, from a sense born in him to recognize his kind from above. He begins a descent, gravity now working with him, and angles in a straight, unwavering line back to where he began. He comes in oblique to the water. The surface speeds beneath him and suddenly he feels his breast collide with the lake. This is landing, this awkward, angled reentry into the water. His momentum takes him a little farther and he stops. He has flown. His parents, the other young loon are diving, going about their business, and he, too, suddenly dives and reenters the green, comfortable depths of the lake, propelling himself down with certainty into the shadowy darkness below.

By the same mysterious calendar that gets chicks hatched in approximately twenty-nine days and human babies born in approximately nine months, both juveniles fly in their eleventh week of life, midway in the range of ten to twelve weeks, during which time most loons can be relied upon to fly.

Their parents stay around a little longer, supplementing the

Yellow Perch

Crayfish

young loons' diets with an extra perch here, a bullhead there. But the adults become increasingly detached, until, one day, they simply do not return. There have been no good-byes, no plans for future meetings; no maps, however mystical and avian, drawn in air, detailed in hoots or kwuks. One evening the sun drops behind the ridge, the darkness unhesitatingly descends on the abandoned young loons, and they are alone for the night. This is how it is. Once the juveniles have achieved flight, the adult loons are ready to leave them to their fate, not knowing nor perhaps caring whether their offspring will ever make it to the ocean, nor whether they will ever return to nest.

For now, the young loons continue on much as they have before — diving, fishing, sleeping mid-lake. Yet flocks of ducks move in during the evenings, splashing down, busily feeding before they're on their way again, and geese fly overhead in long variations on the letter V, honking continuously, maintaining contact in their gradually mutating formations that break like threads, threatening to leave stragglers or whole strings of geese behind. It is mid-October. The lake is now littered with leaves that grow saturated and settle to the bottom. The red and orange festivities are paling; it takes but one night of hard rain and strong wind to strip the trees and change the season. In the morning light the subtleties of winter are revealed — the gunsmoke greys, the subdued browns. On cold nights, ice begins to form on the protected margins of the lake, at first with a rather innocent appearance. But there is danger in this ice. It can gather surface overnight, and suddenly an unsuspecting loon can find there's no way to taxi and get airborne. It is time to go.

The young loons are two of the last of the water birds left on the lake. When the people on shore see them go, they must accept the fact that the earth and especially they themselves are one year older. It seems as though summer just began, and here the loons have gone again for yet another year. Time cycles

round and round, faster and faster, and for some there is a melancholy in the summer's death, a dread that perhaps next year the fish in the lake will be gone. Each summer, seeing the loons thrive is like a gift, a transitory pleasure made all the more acute by its tenuousness. To have seen the loons rear two chicks has made life seem in balance, stable. But with the summer's end there is the realization and the dread that next summer the test will be repeated and their lake may fail. It may be at the coming winter's end that the lake's acidity will have reached the point at which much of the reason for being on the lake — the fishing, the loons, the sense of life to the water — will be absent. It may be that their lake will be the next to turn unnervingly clear, like a swimming pool or an aquarium, attractive to the

unaware, but saddening to the person who experiences this crystalline quality with a sense of profound loneliness, with the grim knowledge that his fellow creatures have gone elsewhere or died and left him to swim alone.

As for the young loons — one morning they head down lake and ascend into the air, pushing against thin air with all their might to raise their bodies and leave behind their natal lake. Anyone watching from shore or from a boat could see them head off as the adult loons did, over the whale-shaped mountains to the south, transformed in a moment from loons, wavering in the air with the exertion of flight, to mere specks, wiggling, growing imperceptibly smaller, until they suddenly blink out of sight and are gone.

AUTUMN -
Migration

By instinct or by chance, the young loons follow a route similar to that taken by their parents weeks before. They do not go far, only a ways over the mountains, over tiny ponds, white from the air, their surfaces already frozen solid. The loons fly until they reach a larger lake, a stopover for loons flying from a wide fan of territory north of it. All across the north, migratory water birds are congregating, seeking out the larger lakes because they have not yet frozen and because their size affords good fishing. Once over the lake, the loons descend, guided by tradition so ingrained in every sinew of their bodies that the water seems to pull them from the sky. They splash down with their rude crash landings and set out paddling to get a sense of the lake, above the surface and below, of the other loons they might encounter, and of the chances for good fishing. Their parents have stopped on the lake, but are no longer there. Along with other adults that have arrived and departed throughout September and October, they have flown on, leaving the younger loons to benefit from fishing without the competition of the older birds.

It is at this point that the young loons that we have watched all summer become indistinguishable among a small group of other juveniles. Their parents have reached the sea, where they

Fringed Gentian

will more than likely winter separately again, having no need to stay in contact with one another outside of the breeding range. Now the two young loons, as well, become simply part of the race of loons, individuals no longer recognizable by their position in a family unit. Not until they return to the breeding range in four years as mature adults ready to find mates will they again become identifiable to the human eye, recognizable because they consistently occupy certain territory and follow predictable patterns within it. Now they have become, for human purposes, simply part of a flock, two of a relatively scant number of juveniles that will replenish the stock on the sea.

✳   ✳   ✳

Salamander

The juveniles remain on the lake only a brief while longer. The flock has been forming for weeks now, gradually, as the surrounding ponds and lakes have yielded the results of the summer; first one young loon, then two, then another, trickling from the mountains like brooks in a dry year. People on shore, with a concern for loons and a knowledge of other years, try to get a count, try to sense if the decline has perhaps been reversed, or if the number of loons reared at least might be similar to last year's. They watch anxiously, like people tallying votes on an issue of high concern. October is drawing to an end, and if, on a smaller lake somewhere in the mountains, a loon is not yet mature enough to fly, its time has about run out.

The days pass, and the young loons grow increasingly restless. They make short flights, like athletes sprinting before a race, calling to one another, using the wail, expressing their need for contact. It is time to go, time to respond to impulses so deep and ancient and tied to the time of year that it is as if the very molecules of the loons are magnetized by the ocean. The loons are motivated by the sum of all loon experience over millions of years — the fresh water has frozen in the past, the salt water hasn't; those loons that have made timely progress to the sea have increased their chances of returning to the north another year. So these descendants of millions of generations of survivors now feel the untried power of their young wings. They are poised to depart, waiting for the conditions to combine that will suddenly carry them, the way a wave suddenly lifts driftwood in surf, and usher them into that unknown skyway that exists between themselves and the sea.

One wonders how they know where to go. Do they orient themselves by means of the sun in the day and by the stars at night? Do they relate themselves to the earth's magnetic field? Do they use landmarks, keeping an eye on the rivers and lakes below, the cities, the mountain ranges, the roads, the coastlines? Do they perhaps use the prevailing winds, the infrared energy rising from the ocean's currents? Most likely they use all these things, or at least a combination of some, particularly the sun and stars and the landmarks on the ground below.

It is believed that loons migrate almost exclusively by day, in common with most large water birds and in contrast to what is perhaps a majority of smaller land birds, who are nocturnal migrants. Using the sun for migration requires the existence of an internal clock, since the position of the sun is only meaningful relative to the hour and time of year, whereas it is thought that nocturnal migrants orient themselves in relation to the configuration of specific constellations or by the fixed position of the North Star. It is perhaps surprising that more birds migrate by night than by day, since darkness eliminates most landmarks on the earth's surface and increases the likelihood of striking obstacles. But, for many birds, other factors figure more importantly, such as having daylight hours free for feeding — capturing insects, gathering seeds.

But even if we could know for sure how young birds orient

The fall migration begins at the end of August or in early September. Prior to migration, loons begin to flock on larger lakes — unsuccessful breeding pairs and unmated birds first, later joined by adults whose young are mature enough to fend for themselves. The juvenile loons are often the last to leave their natal lakes and flock up prior to migration. At the end of September, individuals and small flocks begin to leave the lakes, but often the last loons are not gone until just before a lake freezes over, sometimes as late as November. Along the Atlantic coast, loons can be seen off New England from mid-September into November, arriving in Florida and the Gulf of Mexico from October to mid-November. On the Pacific coast, loons can be found off southern California in mid-October.

themselves, migrating for the first time without the company of adults, there would still remain that even greater mystery — how do they know what destination they are aiming to reach? Or do they even have a sense of destination? Perhaps at each moment they merely respond to a memory born in them, the result of their collective experience as a species that tips a wing here and straightens it out there, accomplishing turns at correct moments that guide the birds by remote control programmed through the ages. Perhaps they merely head south, genetically programmed to fly in that direction, continuing at random until they encounter an environment that matches an image they were born to recognize. Who knows? Perhaps it is a subject best left to those people who don't mind mystery, who feel their imaginations pleasantly released to wander the skies by the sound of a flock of geese passing among the stars or by the sound

of a loon laughing high in the clouds, carrying human thoughts with it north or south through the atmosphere.

∗   ∗   ∗

As the loons make their way south, veering at an angle toward the ocean, they fly over terrain that is dotted with lakes. Resting places, settled predictably into the depressions between countless watersheds, gleam invitingly and are plentiful, offering ample room for takeoff and landing and ample depths for fish. The loons take advantage of them in the evening, splashing down and resting, sometimes spending days, encountering and joining with other loons.

But as the loons continue on, the land below them grows increasingly complex. At first, towns are mere islands in the continuous forest, but as the loons fly on, the right angles, the random gleams that are not water, the grey roads that move with cars, that widen like rivers headed to the sea — two lanes, four lanes, six lanes, eight — increase, gaining dominance, until the colors of grey and black force green into submission, circumscribing it, penning it, and dulling its senses with the gathering haze of smoke. It is not a no-man's-land, this land so claimed by humans, but a land where the black bear is no longer welcome to walk the hills and where a loon is hard pressed to find a safe stretch of water on which to spend the night.

The weather generally warms as the loons fly in a southerly direction, but storms still move in, sometimes just with rain that obscures the sky and land, other times with snow flurries and hail. There is no backtracking to look for a member of the flock that drops out in a storm. If the loons are caught while airborne by a front of inclement weather, each loon is in its own struggle for survival. A loon that grows tired and lags behind is not waited for. If it stops to rest or gets lost, it must find its way alone, unless

Sea Gulls

it picks up with other loons. If it lands on a dark, wet road, mistaking it for a river, it awaits its fate alone, a solitary water bird, feet burned and bruised from the landing, captive of the asphalt, unable to run to pick up speed and fly again. Perhaps it will be found by people understanding enough to return it to a wide body of water, but perhaps, too, it becomes just another casualty of the migration, counted with those that are accidentally or intentionally shot or lost to other causes, or likely never counted at all.

Of course, for some loons that breed near the ocean, the flight is short, sometimes only a matter of hours; but for migrants that have spent many days en route, nearing the coast may well bring with it a sense of relief. Perhaps the loons smell the ocean long before they see it. Perhaps the gulls, wheeling in the air around them, increasing in numbers as the loons near the coast, are a measure of the ocean's proximity. Regardless, finally one day the distant horizon levels in an even, grey-blue band that indicates the loons will soon be in a wilderness as vast as that which they have left. Of course, its surface is crossed by ships, its depths are seined for fish, and from its floor rise mammoth derricks for the drilling of oil, but for the loons it must be a domain that seems infinite and perfectly suited to their needs.

The blue band grows wider, the bold, circling gulls more plentiful, filling the air with their briefly rhythmic, almost raucous calls that so typify the margin of life that edges the oceans. The smell of the water, of decaying sea life, of salt becomes intense, so rich and welcome after passage over the dry land. From the air, land's edge becomes visible with its last frenzy of houses snugged tight to that dividing line between worlds, offering their occupants the stability of solid ground and civilization and the privacy and freedom of a clear, unimpeded horizon. Beyond the houses, there is the beach, that last fraction of the continent where man dare not build. There the ocean's inability to reason defies human bravado, and the houses are kept at bay, the shoreline held in trust by the waves for the tiny sanderlings to probe with their beaks for crabs.

And so they arrive. The dark lines of incoming swells, the rushing edge of white foam increase the loons' appearance of speed as they angle out of the sky, over the waves, to the wide and uninterrupted surface of the ocean. With their first splashdown in salt water, the trip is essentially over. They may fly along the coastline, spreading out, heading farther south, but the dangers of traveling over land have been survived, and the young loons, though they have never been here before, have at last made it home to the sea.

ANOTHER WINTER –
On the ocean

Mackerel

The year has come full circle. The loons are once more on the ocean. As far as the horizon and beyond there is water, perpetually moving, rocking the loons in a rhythm to which they are inherently attuned. Now privacy is easily attained, a wide-open privacy afforded by the very vastness of the ocean. There is ample room for shipping lanes and the insignificant wakes of loons to widen and cross without interference. In the depths there is volume enough for the whales to pass, slow, blue-black, and barnacled, and never impede the loons' descent.

November, December — the days are short, the nights are long and dark. The young loons that we have seen emerge from the walls of their speckled eggs now winter together, kept close by chance and familiarity. They have taken up with a few other loons, occupying a small bay, and at night they raft over the deepest water in its center. Life seems very easy. As it has for millions of years, with each tide the ocean sends new fish shoreward, and the scene, with its foggy greyness, is virtually the same as that where we began — large grey loons rafting at night, fishing by day with a backdrop altered only by changes in the weather.

Just how long the young loons will remain on the ocean before they go inland to breed is not definitely known — three

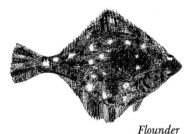

Flounder

Loons generally eat fish under six inches long. Small fish they swallow underwater, but larger fish they surface to swallow. Among the saltwater fish they prey on are: cod, sea trout, herring, flounder, sculpin, surf fish, menhaden, and mackerel.

years, anyway, perhaps four. Occasionally, immature loons are seen inland, passing the summer on freshwater lakes, but for most it is not until their third or fourth spring, when their grey plumage is shed and replaced by the startling patterns of the nuptial plumage, that the young loons will leave the ocean. Then, sexually mature, they will fly north and inland (perhaps even to their natal lake), find mates, and the cycles will be set in motion again, repeating, widening, life upon life like the patterns of raindrops on water.

Or so we hope. Who wants to witness the rearing of chicks over so many months only to have it come to nothing? So let's say, yes, this is what happens. The winter passes, another spring arrives with the mature loons growing restless and leaving the ocean for the north. Summer on the ocean is warm and easy, and with the year's decline once more into autumn, the mature loons return along with new offspring for the year. And so, round and round, winter again, spring, summer, and fall, until the young loons that we have watched finally go inland, separated from one another after at least three long years on the ocean, each seeking his own fate. When they arrive in the north, we will have them each find a lake abundant with fish, and there will be other loons with which to mate and raise their young. Houses will not have usurped their nesting sites. Toxic chemicals will not have affected their fertility or thinned their eggshells. Their chicks, two tiny black ones born to each pair, will be strong and healthy and survive the gauntlet of predators and motorboats.

But how far can we extend our power? By the very act of imagination, can we go on and on for the life of the loons? Can we neutralize the acid rain and keep the water in the lakes sweet and the life there abundant year after year? Can we purify the rivers that flow into the oceans and keep the loons safe from toxic chemicals? Can we prevent radioactive waste on the ocean's floor from leaking, or, darkest question of all, can we hold off nuclear war by pure imagination?

Let's say we can. Let's say our two loons live to old age, possibly twenty, thirty years. It is surmised that loons have an active breeding life of perhaps twelve years, so let's indulge ourselves and, in that time, see the rearing of twenty chicks per pair. Why not? Why should we have followed these chicks all this way just to have them show up in statistics — perhaps a third of juvenile loons lost their first year on the ocean? Let's keep our loons out of the paths of oil spills creeping over the surface of the ocean, occupying more and more area, affecting more and more helpless birds.

Yet, in reality, one begins to wonder if we are helpless. We all know that the birds are victims of our own habits, our own patterns of consumption. The things we use daily — something as common as a plastic bag — figure in a global trade-off. Yet there seems to be no way to make a group decision to curb our habits, our energy use, our intense interest in a seductive array of gadgets, an interest ever renewed by companies working hard to satisfy us, or perhaps working hard to keep us ever unsatisfied.

The problem: how to leave room on this planet for a creature like the loon, a creature we love and value, that, if given a simple choice, we would say we preferred to keep. Through education, law enforcement, zoning, or something as delightfully successful as the nesting platform, it is proving relatively easy to deal with fluctuations of water levels, harassment by boaters, and loss of nesting sites. But the more insidious threats — acid rain, oil spills, nuclear waste, toxic chemicals — are far more difficult to control. Scientific innovation and legislation may not be enough when these problems are fueled by an insatiable demand for energy and for an enormous variety of goods and services that result in the creation of toxic waste. The problem is that, even if we make a personal decision to occasionally say — "No, using this plastic bag is not worth a loon," or "This unnec-

Alewife

Cod

essary trip in the car is not worth a loon" — how do we compound the results sufficiently to make it have any actual impact? Who wants to be the only gloomy soul denying himself pleasures for the sake of a bird approaching extinction, or for the sake of an ecosystem that "can't cope"?

Yet the alternative seems to be to slowly eliminate our fellow species while we ride along on a tide of technological innovations. Even though we know better, our inability to get ahold of ourselves and design a course for the future makes each of us play the fool. It makes us pretend we can have our cake and eat it, too — that we can have nature's delicate beauties and yet live without accommodating them, without giving them room. It makes us individually and collectively irresponsible. We have an eat, drink, and be merry attitude because gadgets are readily available. They add to one's comfort, whereas accommodating a bird like the loon is a difficult chore, with considerable potential for pain and disappointment.

❋　　　❋　　　❋

The year ends in December, with the loons on the sea and the future left unknown. It will not be long before the winter molt begins. The ten long primaries, the wing feathers, will be lost and will drift on the surface of the water; the birds will once again be flightless, in the depth of winter on the ocean. It will be a time as opposite to that moment when a chick struggles free of the egg, when it hears a far-reaching voice issue from the warm body above, as the year will offer. Yet the solstice passes, just before the very end of the year, just before the deepest cold of the winter, and the sun starts north, daily trimming the darkness. It is December. The year has ended, but already a new year inches into existence.

PART II
The History

THE HISTORY

I want to convey to you how long loons have existed, and then I wonder why. What does it matter that loons are the oldest birds in North America and one of the oldest birds on earth? A buttercup is no better or more interesting than a lily just because it evolved earlier. Yet the figure sixty million years seems as significant to me as does the loon's unforgettable call or its startling beauty.

Stop and think . . . sixty million years. We are used to much larger figures — deficits, miles into space, government spending, human population. The numbers roll off the tongue with ease. Yet we deal with the convenience of lump sums. The miles are not walked, the dollars not counted, the people not assembled. It is easy to read in print that loons have existed sixty million years, but I believe the significance of this figure lies in the effect it has on our minds when we begin to truly grasp just how long these birds have been on earth. It affects the way we feel when the calls reach our ears from out of the darkness, or when we see the precision of the black and white breeding plumage laid down on the back of yet another individual. And it gives us another way to look at ourselves. It increases our sense of our relationship and continuity with nature.

But how do we fathom the past of a bird that has repeated

Indian Cucumber Root

the same yearly cycle over and over sixty million times? How do we distinguish one year from the next? How do we count the number of times the long winter on the sea has given way to spring, how many times the loons have migrated north to mate and nest and raise their young? How do we comprehend how long loons have been paddling the lakes, watching for fish, diving and resurfacing, or how many times they have made the autumn migration to the ocean to winter again? How do we comprehend how many tiny black chicks, smaller than your fist when they first enter the water, have linked past with future so that loons might endure?

Maybe the simplest way to envision this span of years is with a time line. We can draw a line six inches long to represent sixty million years, but it will represent the same unbroken existence with equal inscrutability unless we mark it with divisions.

LOONS ——— PEOPLE

So let's use our own existence as a reference point. Each inch on the line represents ten million years. To the left we will write in the word "loons" horizontally, because there is plenty of room, but then we must move all the way over to the last tenth of an inch on the right, to the last one sixtieth of the line, before we write in vertically the word "people." This is giving us one million years, not a stingy allotment, but wedged into that narrow space are all sorts of rough and hairy types, beginning with the first true man, *Homo erectus* or "standing man," whose principal accomplishment was merely to get off all fours and thus have his hands free to throw things and swing clubs. In order to encounter people able to use fire, for instance, we must move to the last one three-hundredth of the line, where we meet ape-like Java man with his heavy brows and hairy body. And in the tiny segment that is left, we have yet to squeeze in the Neanderthals, the Ice Ages, and *Homo sapiens*. In a virtually microscopic speck of the loons' total existence the wheel must be invented, the first alphabet developed, and the giant pyramids hauled, rock by rock, into existence.

But what about Columbus? What about the Pilgrims and the settling of America? With just a little change of perspective, it is quite easy to think this all took place a long time ago. However, the Pilgrims set up camp thirty-five millionths of an inch from the end of the line; the forests were yet to be cleared, the plains divided, the Revolutionary and Civil wars yet to be fought, our cities yet to rise glittering from the earth. Is it any wonder that loons so often look at us with startled surprise? After sixty million years, who are these newcomers with such power, energy, and numbers who were not here such a very little time ago?

LOONS

Now that we have some sense of proportion, of the scale of things, let's go back and look at just what *did* go on for those fifty-nine million years before our remotest arrival.

＊   ＊   ＊

Loons appear in geologic remains relatively soon after the demise of the great dinosaurs at the end of the Mesozoic era. The dinosaurs came to a very abrupt end for reasons that are still unclear — volcanic activity, earthquakes, the collision of an asteroid with earth — something caused the climate to cool, and

THE PILGRIMS
COLUMBUS
THE PYRAMIDS
THE WHEEL
HOMO SAPIENS
THE ICE AGES
NEANDERTHAL MAN
HOMO ERECTUS

Archaeopteryx, *the first true bird,
lived one hundred and fifty million
years ago. It was descended from
reptiles that took to the trees as a
means of survival during the reign of
the dinosaurs. It had the first true
feathers (evolved from reptilian
scales) and birdlike feet, yet it still
retained lizardlike claws, extending
from its wings, and a mouth full of
sharp teeth.*

the huge, cold-blooded beasts were too accustomed to consistently warm conditions to readily adapt. Being big eaters, they could not scurry around and make do.

So the stage was cleared for new life forms to take dominance, and, with the beginning of the present era of geologic time, the Cenozoic, we see the sudden flourishing of mammals, insects, and birds, no longer held in check by the dinosaurs' massive presence.

Up until this time, birds had not evolved very far. They had descended from small reptiles that took to the trees as a means of survival, resulting, one hundred and fifty million years ago, in the first true bird. *Archaeopteryx* was a crow-sized creature that had evolved feathers over its entire body, perhaps due to chillier temperatures in the shade of the treetops or to enable it to glide effectively to the ground. It still was quite reptilian, with toes and claws extending rather bizarrely from the ends of its wings, but its nose was decidedly beak-shaped, and it had developed two other important birdlike characteristics — warm blood and opposable toes, the latter of which enabled it to grasp branches like a perching bird.

It is hard to be sure what kind of birds succeeded *Archaeopteryx*. There may be no record of some land birds, but, due to the fact that bones deposited in mud are quite readily preserved, there is a good record of two sea birds that lived about seventy million years ago, one of particular interest in tracing the development of loons. They are *Ichthyornis*, a small and able flier resembling an early tern, and *Hesperornis*, an enormous diving bird, six feet long, extraordinarily similar in structure to present-day loons. An interesting feature of *Hesperornis* is that it was flightless. Flight is an expensive means of survival. That is, it requires an incredible amount of energy for a bird to occupy the domain of air. Thus *Hesperornis* probably abandoned the use of wings, because life in and under water adequately supplied its daily needs. This is also partially true of loons today. Their exceptional ability underwater is the counterpart of a reduced dependence on flight.

It is believed that no animals over fifty pounds survived the end of the Mesozoic era. As a result, the earliest evolution at the dawn of the Cenozoic era, sixty-five million years ago, was toward gigantism, to fill the empty niches with intimidating creatures like the "terror crane," a massive land bird, nine feet tall and with a head the size of a horse's. As the Cenozoic era progressed, however, things started to settle down and more familiar kinds of life forms began to evolve. Due to the cooler temperatures, grasses became the dominant form of vegetation, and the mammals, which until then had been small and mousey, gradually developed into larger grazing animals. It is at this point that we encounter the first relatives of elephants, horses, rhinoceroses, and pigs.

It is also at this time that we encounter the first loons. One always reconstructs a picture of geologic time on a hypothetical basis, since no one can ever be sure which skeletons got mixed up with which and what animals never got fossilized. Nevertheless, from what is surmised of the animals living sixty million years ago, one could imagine a picture of loons nesting in tall grasses at the edge of a lake visited, not by moose and white-tailed deer, but by *Brontotherium*, a double-horned, eight-foot North American rhinoceros, or *Orohippus*, a little sixteen-inch relative of the horse. On the ocean, one can imagine loons floating on the surface of the water, most likely with half an eye out for *Basilosaurus* — a mammal that took to the sea, a primitive relative of whales, eighty feet long, a carnivore with a huge mouth of sharp teeth. What birds may have occupied the early Cenozoic era with loons is a matter of even greater speculation, since most birds have hollow bones, which are easily decomposed before fossilization can occur. It seems that cormorants,

Hesperornis *lived seventy million years ago, and although the loon is not considered a direct descendant, there are remarkable similarities between the two.* Hesperornis *was a foot-propelled diver, with feet set far to the rear of its heavy body. Its considerable proficiency underwater resulted in the loss of its ability to fly, as is clear from the fossilized remains of its diminutive wings and enormous, six-foot body.*

Brontotherium

gulls, and vultures were the earliest species, followed in the next twenty million years by representatives of most of the other families of birds.

This gives you a general picture of the Cenozoic era as it progressed toward the present. Through warming and cooling trends, species came and went, and the face of the planet began to take on an increasingly familiar look. But by looking at the time line again, one realizes that man is still quite far in the future. For most of the Cenozoic era our ancestors, the primates, were little more than monkeys in the trees. It was not until just

five million years ago that an ape descended to the ground with
the rudiments of human form, and, as we know, he was well in
advance of the appearance of *Homo sapiens*.

*   *   *

There is a final segment to this history. But let's begin it with
one concept in mind. It has become a common saying that loons
are "symbols of wilderness." This is because the loon, being shy
of humans, has secluded itself in the most private corners of the
north, pushed back like wilderness itself, into the most rugged
and inaccessible areas. What is interesting is that the loon was no
less a symbol of wilderness in the past. Throughout the settling
of North America the loon has represented all that is wild and
unknown. As a result, it has been subjected to very uneven
treatment, because regard for the loon has fluctuated with people's attitudes toward nature.

The early Eskimos and Indians seem to have had a fairly
stable relationship with loons, as they did with their environments. Neither group existed in large enough numbers to have
much impact, nor did they hunt loons to any appreciable extent
for food, using them only occasionally in making clothes and in
ornamentation. Loons, being fish eaters, unlike most ducks and
geese, have always had in their favor the fact that their meat is
fishy tasting; so, for the earliest human inhabitants of this continent, uninclined to kill just for sport, the loon remained more of a
godlike presence: the spirit of a warrior denied entry into heaven
for the Cree; the most handsome of birds for the Ojibways; an
omen of death for the Chipewyans. It is easy to imagine what
might well have been a long-lasting state of peaceful coexistence.

The white settlers set foot on the North American continent
with no such feeling of well-being, however. The sea of trees was
not home and far from it. The process of civilization had taken

humans out of the wilderness in Europe, and these people were unprepared to reenter it with ease. Yet, for many of them, passage back to their homeland was not an option, so striking off to make sense of life in these new conditions was the only choice. What the early settler did not need, as he braved virgin forests of towering trees, where even the smallest clearing was hard won and neighbors were nowhere to be found, was some strange, bloodcurdling voice coming out of the distance, reminding him of all he did not know about his new home. One might well imagine that loons came to be looked upon negatively at that very first encounter.

By the mid-1800s the wilderness had by and large been conquered. It was well mapped, traversed by roads, and regarded with a growing sense of proprietorship, a confident sense that resources existed for human use. The attitude toward loons did not improve with this new outlook. Fishermen got nervous when they saw loons surface with shining fish and feed them to chicks, as they had done for millions of years. The men looked on the fish as their own and the loons as thieves. Thus it became easy to justify shooting a loon on sight, not for food, but just to be rid of it, to eliminate the competition. Unfortunately, it would be a long time before biologists studying the loon's diet would inform fishermen that loons were feeding predominately on less desirable species and thereby improving conditions for the choicer game fish.

This situation continued well into the twentieth century, as did another, even more devastating one. By the early 1900s the wilderness was beginning to be looked upon as a source of entertainment and pleasure. A few dangers still lurked there. Bears and panthers were still plentiful. But civilization had gotten enough of an upper hand that it became stylish for even women and children to venture out into the great tracts of northern evergreens. Elegant lakeside hotels were established, and big

steamers conveyed city people over the water for vacations. The loon's downfall at this time was the way in which its very entertaining ability at diving appealed to people's new sense of play. As people stood on the decks of the big steamers, idly awaiting arrival at the hotels, they became fascinated with the way the loons, fearing danger or merely fishing, would abruptly disappear beneath the surface, swim in totally unpredictable directions at astonishing speeds, and resurface when and where the observers least expected. The air of vacation lightheartedness, combined with an attitude that nature was at last at man's disposal, led people to get out their guns and turn the steamer rides into shooting matches, with the result that, on some lakes, the arrival of the big boats was heralded by barrages of gunfire.

At this same time, the early 1900s, loons were suffering from exposure to humans at another point in their yearly cycle. After wintering on the ocean, each spring the loons flew north along the Atlantic coast. To this day, this route is a major flyway for an enormous number of species, but until the early part of this century the birds flew unprotected by any legislation. It is a peculiarity of the coastline that when the flocks reach Cape Cod they fly up Buzzards Bay and along the channel rather than going around the peninsula. This convenient chance of geography provided the ideal setup for marksmen to practice their shooting early each spring, and the banks of the channel were annually lined with people indiscriminately bringing down, but not retrieving, whatever flew by.

Needless to say, with this sort of attitude present in the country, it was not too long before the concept of scarcity entered people's vocabularies with regard to certain wild creatures. This new awareness was reinforced dramatically when, in 1914, the last of the passenger pigeons died in a Cincinnati zoo. This may not seem significant if one does not know that the passenger pigeon was a wild bird that once lived in North America in

Passenger Pigeon

such enormous numbers that flocks literally hundreds of miles long and miles wide were common. John James Audubon once reported seeing a flock so dense that it shut out the sunlight for three days as it passed overhead. Through most of the nineteenth century, however, an insatiable market existed for squabs and pigeons and they were shot and netted without restraint, despite the Indians' pleas for moderation. Sophisticated rifles and railroad lines made for devastating efficiency of extermination and shipping, and by the end of the nineteenth century the pigeons were almost gone. In the early part of the twentieth century, people began to wonder about the "mystery" of the disappearance of the passenger pigeon. One can't help thinking they knew what had happened, and that this created a new germ of conscience from which other species, including the loon, would benefit.

It is at this time, in the year 1914, as a matter of fact, that the Weeks-McLean Migratory Bird Law was passed in the United States. By 1918, this law had gone into full effect as the Migratory Bird Treaty Act, under which nearly all migratory nongame birds, including the loon, are protected to this day. After the passage of this bill, the loons' dwindling numbers slowly began to restabilize.

With the start of the First World War in 1914, use of the automobile increased. Roads were improved, and the efficiency and economy of the automobile became widely appealing. The result for wilderness and for loons was that people, as they steadily increased in numbers, further extended their reach over the continent of North America.

The abundance of wilderness was adequate to absorb this expansion for a considerable amount of time, but by the fifties this new mobility was to gravely affect the loon. Until this time, many northern lakes were included in the land-holdings of large farms. As individual mobility increased, a demand grew for private wilderness retreats. Thus, it became economically advantageous for farmers to sell lakeshore property for the construction of second homes.

The effect on loons was at first gradual, but by the seventies people began to realize that something was wrong. Lakes where loons had nested for as long as anyone could remember were suddenly abandoned by the birds. People who had initiated child after child into the wilderness, sitting beside them in the darkness listening to the loons' calls, now waited in vain. There was bitter irony in this, for loons, above all, symbolized the qualities that people were seeking in wilderness. Yet the loons were not and are not returning to many lakes.

And so we are brought up to the present, having traced a history that began sixty million years ago. The loon is suffering from loss of habitat due to lakeshore development. It is threat-

Green Frog

ened by both deliberate and inadvertent harassment by boaters and canoeists. It must contend with water-level fluctuations due to flood control and electrical power generation on man-made lakes, to name but a few of the modern obstacles to its continued existence. Yet, once discovered, these obstacles are proving relatively manageable. Through research and education of the public, it seems possible to accommodate the loons' basic needs for suitable nesting sites and relative privacy.

Unfortunately, the situation is not that simple. It seems that the seventies and the eighties, such a minute segment of loon history, have ushered in yet another phase. Wilderness was here before man. We entered it, we were overwhelmed, but we conquered it. Now, however, we are faced with the bewildering prospect that we, ourselves, have become overwhelming — not in obvious ways, as when we indulged in overkill of migratory birds at the beginning of the century, but in bafflingly insidious ways that are deeply disturbing and hard to remedy. Oil spills are one example of this. They are devastating to loons on the winter range. Mercury poisoning is another, accounting for the loss of twenty-five hundred loons on the Gulf coast in 1983 alone. Botulism, toxic waste, pesticides commonly take their toll. But perhaps the most direct threat of all, the one which may bring this long history to an abrupt halt within the decade of the eighties, is acid rain. For a fish-eating bird like the loon, it is a formidable obstacle to survival. In the Adirondacks, by 1984, two hundred lakes were listed as officially dead. In Ontario the toll was higher, over one thousand lakes lifeless. Once a lake dies, the loons go elsewhere — until there is nowhere else to go.

Thus, just as we are prepared to play the role of stewards of wilderness, inspired with reverence for a shrinking cause, suddenly the balance is tipping to the point where we may not even have the option to kindly foster nature's existence. The reason is this, I believe. Nature, the wild, call it what you will — the complex web of life on this planet, which has been in the making for over three billion years — will never be something we can manage. We can help it to survive, as we do the loon with the building of artificial nesting platforms or the shepherding of families with small chicks, but ultimately, unless we manage ourselves in order to simply give nature room to take care of itself, all of our best efforts will be useless. All of our highest computer technology will never be adequate to track and trace all of the bug trails, all of the worm meanderings, all of the bird trajectories with which our lives are intertwined. And once the web is broken, a web that has been in the loom so long that even loons look like newcomers, then we may see our whole environ- ment succumb in the same microscopic speck of time as the loon.

APPENDIX

LANGUAGE OF THE LOON

This information was adapted from the record album "Voices of the Loon," by William Barklow, copyright 1980, published by the North American Loon Fund and the National Audubon Society.

Though the Common Loon's ability at vocalization is one of its most noticeable characteristics, its repertoire of calls is surprisingly small compared with that of some songbirds. For this reason, it has been possible for people to begin to analyze the meanings of the different calls the loon makes. In the years that people have been listening to loons and imagining the meanings of their calls, there have, of course, been countless interpretations as to just what the loons are saying. For a long time, for instance, the wail was said to be an indicator of rain. Though this does not seem to be borne out by experience (loons in summer may utter the wail nightly, while a week may pass without rain), who can ultimately question the instinctive interpretation of a longtime loon-listener who has listened soul to soul to the loons for decades? The meanings given here are those being developed by ornithologists, and, while they are based on empirical evidence, something as infinite as the calling of loons defies conclusive lexicography.

One aspect of loon behavior that runs counter to the assignment of strict meanings to their calls is chorusing. On a lake large enough to support numerous loons, there will be nights when the tremolos or wails of one individual will be picked up and repeated by other loons, until the darkness is charged with excitement. It is hard to imagine what the loons are expressing with such collective vocalization. To the human ear, it can sound either unnerving or reassuringly vital. Whatever the motivation, it certainly is not the sound of one loon making deliberate and seemingly reasoned expression to another.

Loons call infrequently, if at all, in winter, but in summer their vocalizations play an important role, as the loons make contact with one another, defend their territories, and care for their young. Four basic calls have been defined, in addition to the nearly continuous peeping of young chicks. An expanded use of these four calls becomes possible when volume and pitch are altered, phrases repeated, or one call combined with another.

THE WAIL

The wail is the most frequently heard call of the loon. It is a location call, used when one loon is trying to locate another. It is often uttered at night, when it more than likely indicates that one loon of a pair is ready to give up nest duties. Less frequently, it is also used to contact a chick, but in this case it might be preceded by the tremolo, which would give the wail an added connotation of anxiety. The wail is a very loud call, capable of carrying for miles, so it is surprising that it is uttered with the bill nearly closed. The significance of the call can be made more intense by a raise in pitch and the addition of extra "syllables."

THE TREMOLO

The tremolo may indicate alarm, usually due to disturbance by either a human, a predator, or another loon. The call resembles human laughter, yet when one realizes that it indicates distress and fear, this "laughter" quickly takes on an unsettling quality. The tremolo is heard early in spring in territorial defense and later in defense of the nest or chicks. It consists of anywhere from three to ten notes uttered rapidly and evenly. As with the wail, the intensity of the call's meaning is increased by alteration of the pitch and the addition of extra sets of notes.

The tremolo is the only call made in flight. It is also the call most frequently combined with another. When thus combined, two feelings are expressed. The tremolo-wail indicates fear (tremolo) plus desire for contact (wail), as we have seen when a mature loon might be trying to drive off a threat to a chick she very much wants to reach. The tremolo-yodel would likely be used in a territorial dispute where a male is afraid but trying to drive off another male. In this case, the tremolo indicates fear while the yodel indicates aggression.

THE YODEL

The yodel is by far the most complex utterance of the loon. It is actually a song, not a call, in that it is used in the identification and defense of territory. It is most frequently heard in spring and early summer. The yodel consists of a slow, rising note followed by several undulating phrases. The intensity of the aggression is expressed in the number of times the undulations are repeated.

One aspect of the yodel that is exciting for the future of loon biology is that each male seems to have a slightly different version of this call, identifiable from year to year. Loons are very difficult to band because they are strong and elusive and because ornithologists simply hate to disturb a bird that is already suffering from the effects of human encroachment. Through the use of recordings, however, it is possible to identify individual males, to determine if they are returning to the same lakes annually, and to monitor their particular patterns of behavior throughout the summer months.

THE HOOT

The hoot or "kwuk," as it is sometimes called, is that very intimate talking sound that loons make. It sounds very private compared with the loon's other calls, but actually it can carry surprisingly far, for all its softness of tone. The hoot is a one-syllable call with various pitches, each of which probably has a different meaning. It is used to maintain contact between mated pairs and with chicks.

TYPES OF NESTS

Loon nests show considerable variation, depending on their location and the availability of building materials. One common type of nest is built on an island or promontory near an open expanse of water. The nest generally is not more than five feet from the water and is protected by vegetation. It contains whatever plants are handy, both aquatic and land, including sedge, moss, ferns, cattails, and miscellaneous twigs. Its size is usually quite large, averaging twenty-two inches outside diameter and thirteen inches inside diameter, with a depth of three inches.

Occasionally, when vegetation is not available, the nest will be little more than a scraped depression in the sand. The amount of vegetation added to a nest may also be influenced by whether it is the second nest the loons have built that season. Often a second nest may be smaller due to lack of time.

Another common type of nest occurs in marshy areas. It frequently is built on an already existing hummock of vegetation, a muskrat house or floating bog material, to which the loons add, creating a dense, interwoven container contoured to their own breasts. Nests such as these are often surprisingly damp, a condition aggravated by fluctuating water levels, but the heat generated by the adult loons is generally sufficient to keep the eggs warm, unless the nest is flooded.

The artificial nesting platform is a man-made device. Built of cedar posts with a wire mesh base and anchored with cement blocks, this floating island is covered with sod and a collection of indigenous vegetation. As predators such as raccoons become more prevalent and traditional island nesting sites are usurped by human inhabitants, the artificial nesting platform, with its ability to rise and fall with fluctuating water levels, has become a vital tool in preserving the loon.

Scrape

Hummock

Artificial nesting platform

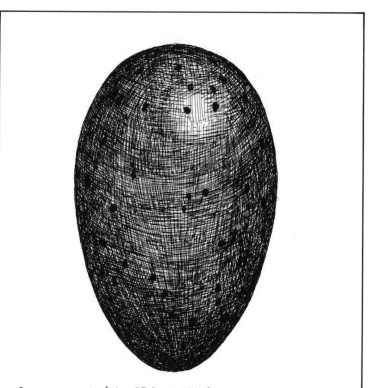

Loon egg — actual size: 87.5mm x 55.6 mm

EGGS

Loons generally lay two eggs per pair per summer. Some clutches are observed with only a single egg, though this may actually be due to the loss of the other egg. It has been reported that three-egg clutches exist, but this is poorly documented. The eggs are generally laid two days apart. They are oval, about the size of goose eggs, and vary in color from olive green to brownish. They are sometimes plain, but usually are covered with small brown speckles.

ENVIRONMENTAL THREATS

ACID RAIN

Of all the dangers that loons face, perhaps none poses a greater threat than acid rain. Acid rain affects loons in several ways. Acids, produced in the atmosphere due to emissions from coal-fired power plants, factories, and automobiles (to name a few of the primary sources), fall to earth and mobilize naturally occurring metals in the soil. These metals, washed down streams and into lakes, are toxic not only to fish, on which loons depend for food, but even directly to loons themselves. Mercury, for instance, may be at first harmlessly stored away in the loon's body fat, but then, in times of stress, when the fat is needed for survival, this mercury is released with deadly effect.

Across the northern United States and Canada, lake after lake has been rendered clear and lifeless due to the presence of heavy metals in its water. The statistics make one pause. Stone flies and mayflies, which are essential for the breakdown of vegetative matter, disappear at pH 5. At pH 5.5, bass, walleyes, and rainbow trout are eliminated. With median pH for precipitation in the Northeast measured at 4.3 in 1984, and considering the limited ability of the soil to neutralize the acids, it is not hard to see that there is a problem.

OIL SPILLS

Oil spills are alarming, in part due to the resulting loss of bird life. A loon caught in an oil spill can be affected in a variety of ways, most of them fatal. Oil is toxic, and a loon attempting to clean itself is likely to swallow lethal amounts. Also, oil breaks down the loon's natural barrier against the cold by clogging its feathers' barbs and destroying natural protective oils. Once sea water is admitted into the fluffy down of the loon, the bird becomes chilled, may develop pneumonia, and may actually become waterlogged and sink, never to be counted among the casualties of an oil spill.

Major accidents are not the only sources of oil on the oceans. There are numerous unpublicized smaller spills, and even more significant is the common practice of tankers routinely flushing oil from their holds to clean them. In fact, it is estimated that twice as much oil is released via dirty ballast than in accidental spills.

PESTICIDES AND TOXIC CHEMICALS

Unlike birds such as the peregrine falcon and the brown pelican, the Common Loon seems minimally affected by pesticides such as DDT and DDD. While eggshell thinning has been recorded, it does not yet seem to be at levels that are likely to cause loss of embryos.

As the amount of PCBs released into the ocean from the production of plastics, paints, and oily lubricants increases, however, an entirely different threat to sea life is developing, as these pollutants become stored in the tissues of birds like the loon.

BIBLIOGRAPHY

"Acid Precipitation," *Mother Earth News*, 73 (January-February, 1982), 122-124.

Baker, Robin. *The Mystery of Migration*. New York: Viking Press, 1980.

Barklow, William. "Voices of the Loon" (record). Meredith, New Hampshire: North American Loon Fund, 1980.

Barnett, Lincoln. *The Ancient Adirondacks*. Alexandria, Virginia: Time-Life, 1974.

Bartlett, Jen and Des. "Diary of a Loon Watcher," *International Wildlife*, 11 (January-February, 1981), 40-48.

Bent, Arthur C. *Life Histories of North American Diving Birds*. New York: Dover Publications, Inc., 1919.

Bernard, C. J. *Animal Behavior: Ecology and Evolution*. New York: Wiley-Interscience, 1983.

Berthold, Peter, and Querner, Ulrich. "Genetic Basis of Migratory Behavior in European Warblers," *Science*, 212 (April 3, 1981), 77-78.

Boyle, Robert H., and Boyle, R. Alexander. *Acid Rain*. New York: Schocken Books, 1983.

Bull, John, and Farrand, John, Jr. *The Audubon Society Field Guide to North American Birds: Eastern Region*. New York: Alfred A. Knopf, 1977.

Fichtel, Chris. "Loons, the Call of the Wild," *Vermont Life,* 38 (Summer, 1984), 32-35.

Freethy, Ron. *How Birds Work — A Guide to Bird Biology*. Poole, Dorset, England: Blanford Books, Ltd., 1982.

Graham, F., Jr. "Mystery at Dog Island," *Audubon*, 86 (March, 1984), 30-33.

Griffin, Donald R. *Bird Migration*. Garden City, New York: Anchor Books, 1964.

Hammond, David E., and Wood, Rawson L. *New Hampshire and The Disappearing Loon*. Center Harbor, New Hampshire: Loon Preservation Committee, 1976.

Kirshner, Ralph. *The Common Loon on Lake Winnipesaukee*. Center Harbor, New Hampshire: The Lake Winnipesaukee Association and the Loon Preservation Committee, 1976.

Knox, Richard A. "Calls of the Wild," *Boston Globe Magazine* (May 22, 1983), p. 14-38.

Koenig, Peter. "Remember the Amoco Cadiz," *Audubon*, 83 (March, 1981), 102-112.

LaBastille, Anne. "The Endangered Loon," *Adirondack Life* (May-June, 1977).

Lewin, Roger. *The Thread of Life: The Smithsonian Looks at Evolution*. Washington, D.C.: Smithsonian Books, 1982.

Lincoln, Frederick C. *The Migration of American Birds*. New York: Doubleday, Doran and Co., Inc., 1939.

McCormick, John. *The Life of the Forest*. New York: McGraw-Hill Book Co., 1966.

McIntyre, Anthony, and Judith W. "Spots Before Your Eyes, an Aid to Identifying Wintering Loons," *Auk*, 91 (April, 1974), 413-415.

McIntyre, Judith W. "Biology and Behavior of the Common Loon (*Gavia immer*) with Reference to its Adaptability in a Man-Altered Environment." Unpublished Doctoral thesis, Department of Zoology, University of Minnesota, 1976.

McLoughlin, John C. *The Tree of Animal Life: A Tale of Changing Forms and Fortunes*. New York: Dodd Mead and Co., 1981.

Marcus, Steven J. "Acid Rain: Technologies Exist to Flush the Problem Away," *Audubon*, 83 (March, 1981), 120-123.

Marshall, Alexandra. *Still Waters*. New York: William Morrow and Company, Inc., 1978.

Mathisen, John E. "Use of Man-made Islands as Nesting Sites for the Common Loon," *Wilson Bulletin*, 81 (September, 1969), 331.

Olson, S. T., and Marshall, W. H. *The Common Loon in Minnesota*. Minnesota Museum of Natural History, Occasional Papers No. 5, 1952.

Palmer, Ralph S. (ed.). *Handbook of North American Birds*. Vol. I, New Haven, Connecticut: Yale University Press, 1962.

Pearson, T. Gilbert. *Birds of America*. Garden City, New York: Doubleday and Company, Inc., 1936.

Peterson, Roger Tory, and McKenny, Margaret. *A Field Guide to Wildflowers of Northeastern and North-Central North America*. Boston: Houghton Mifflin Co., 1974.

Peterson, Roger Tory. "The Loon." New York: National Audubon Society, 1941.

Pistorius, Alan. "Feathering the Loon's Nest," *Country Journal*, 6 (May, 1979), 42-46.

Pittman, James A. "Observations of Loon Air Flight Speed," *Wilson Bulletin*, 65 (June, 1953), 213.

Popisil, Allan. "The Loon Rangers Ride Again," *New England Monthly,* 1 (July, 1984), 30-36.

Ream, Catherine H. "Loon Productivity, Human Disturbance and Pesticide Residues in Northern Minnesota," *Wilson Bulletin*, 88 (September, 1976), 427-432.

Ridgely, Robert. "The Common Loon on Squam Lake," *New Hampshire Audubon Quarterly,* 28 (Spring, 1975), 30-52.

Robbins, Chandler S., Bruun, Bertel, and Zim, Herbert S. *Birds of North America: A Guide to Field Identification.* Revised edition. New York: Golden Press, 1983.

Rossman, George, Allen, and Bob. *The Loon.* Grand Rapids, Minnesota: *Grand Rapids Herald-Review,* 1967.

Rummel, Linda, and Goetzinger, Charles. "The Communication of Intraspecific Aggression in the Common Loon," *Auk,* 92 (April, 1975), 333-346.

Scott, Peter (ed.). *The World Atlas of Birds.* New York: Crescent Books, 1974.

Sjolander, Sverre, and Agren, Greta. "Reproductive Behavior of the Common Loon," *Wilson Bulletin,* 84 (September, 1972), 296-308.

Southern, William E. "Copulatory Behavior of the Common Loon," *Wilson Bulletin,* 73 (September, 1961), 280.

Spinar, Zdenek V. *Life Before Man.* New York: Crescent Books, 1972.

Steele, Frederic L. *Trees and Shrubs of Northern New England.* Concord, New Hampshire: Society for the Protection of New Hampshire Forests, 1971.

Sutcliffe, Scott A., and LaBaron, Geoff. *The Common Loon on Squam Lake.* Plymouth, New Hampshire: Squam Lake Association, 1976.

Sutcliffe, Scott A. (ed.). *The Common Loon — Proceedings of the Second North American Conference on Common Loon Research and Management.* New York: National Audubon Society, 1979.

Sutton, George M. *Water, Prey and Game Birds of North America.* Ed. Alexander Wetmore. Washington, D.C.: National Geographic Society, 1965.

Tate, D. Jean, and James, Jr. "Mating Behavior of the Common Loon," *Auk* 87 (January, 1970), 125-130.

Terres, John K. *Audubon Society Encyclopedia of North American Birds.* New York: Alfred A. Knopf, 1980.

Vermeer, Kees. "Some Aspects of Nesting Requirements of Common Loons in Alberta," *Wilson Bulletin,* 85 (December, 1973), 429-435.

Wilson, Frank N. "The Loon at Close Range," *Bird Lore,* 31 (March-April, 1929), 95-104.

Woolfenden, Glen E. "Selection for a Delayed Simultaneous Wing Molt in Loons," *Wilson Bulletin,* 79 (December, 1967), 416-420.